Husband Leadership Principles

By

Dr. Derrick L. Campbell

Copyright © 2016 By Derrick L. Campbell

All rights reserved. No part of this book may be reproduced in any form or by any electronic or mechanical means, including information storage and retrieval systems, without permission in writing from the publisher, except by a reviewer who may quote brief passages in a review.

All Scriptures included and referred to in the text are from the King James translation of the Holy Bible.

Published by
Derrick L. Campbell
PO Box 4707
Cherry Hill, New Jersey 08034
info@thepromisedlandmnistry.com
Visit our website @ www.thepromisedlandministry.com

First edition: May 2016

ISBN: 978-0-9975052-0-7

Printed in the United States of America

TABLE OF CONTENTS

Page

About the Author v

Introduction 1

Chapter 1. The Husband Leadership Challenge 5

Chapter 2. The VC^{3}S Leadership Model 9

Chapter 3. Husband Leadership Principle #1 17

Chapter 4. Husband Leadership Principle #2 41

Chapter 5. Husband Leadership Principle #3 143

Chapter 6. Husband Leadership Principle #4 163

Chapter 7. Husband Leadership Principle #5 211

ABOUT THE AUTHOR

Dr. Campbell holds a Bachelor of Science degree in Electronics Engineering Technology from Capital Institute of Technology, a second Bachelor of Science degree in Math Education from the University of the District of Columbia, a Masters in Education Administration from Lincoln University, and a doctoral degree in Educational Leadership from Rowan University.

He is also the founder and CEO of DLC Consultant Group. After authoring his first book, Promoting Positive Racial Teacher-Student Classroom Relationships, in January 2008, Dr. Campbell developed a Cultural Relationship Training Program that improves teacher-student classroom relationships as well as several companion programs. He also developed the B.O.S.S. Leadership Training Program that improves manager-employee workplace relationships and relationships between Law Enforcement and their local community.

Dr. Campbell is founder and president of The Promised Land Ministry. The Promised Land Ministry provides training for churches and non-profit organizations. Churches and non-profit organizations receive training in the areas of strategic planning, team building, and leadership.

In August 2007, Dr. Campbell founded Leadership Advancement Journal which publishes articles on recent educational, organizational, and business developments that impact our culture. His articles, Reducing Cultural Bullying in Schools and Reducing Inappropriate Special Education Referrals for Historically Underserved Students, have been featured in a local New Jersey newspaper.

In November 2008, Dr. Campbell began the new Radio talk show - Culturally Speaking with Doctor Derrick. On this talk show we discussed the solutions to the cultural challenges that exist in our schools, workplaces, and community. Dr. Campbell has had a host of local and national speakers who contributed to the content of the show.

Dr. Campbell authored his second book, Leading Your Marriage into the Promised Land, in February 2009. Leading Your Marriage into the Promised Land book helps couples to better work together as a team and eliminate conflict in the marriage. Following the writing of this book, he wrote two companion workbooks, one for husbands and the other for wives.

In September 2014, he authored Advanced Marriage Training for Singles. This book guides singles to determine where God has called them to serve so that they may make a better choice in choosing a potential spouse.

In March 2016, he authored Advanced Marriage Training for Couples workbook. The workbook accompanies the workshop where couples learn their god ordained purpose, how to infuse agape love into their marriage, and how to build a God purposed marriage.

Dr. Campbell has lectured at various locations throughout the nation, including the National Association for the Advancement of Colored People (NAACP), Iron Sharpens Iron Men's Conference, and local churches. He has ministered to the youth at his home church on the topic of Christian student rights in the public schools and has ministered at other local New Jersey church on Overcoming the Poverty Cycle. He has been a board member of his church's men's ministry, Athletes United in Christ, and has participated in various church activities. He was a board member for several non-profit organizations. He has facilitated Leading Your Marriage into the Promised seminars and Advanced Marriage Training for Couples at churches and the Iron Sharpens Iron Conference Men's Conference.

Dr. Campbell is available for speaking engagements.

Introduction

A man who becomes a husband faces many obstacles during his life. Many of these obstacles help to define our purpose and personalities as well as our viewpoints regarding marriage. How we overcome those dictate the type of leaders we are in the home.

The story of Joseph provides an example of a man who faced many obstacles and was able to maintain a healthy marriage. Joseph's brothers hated him so much that they abandoned him, which resulted in him being sold into slavery. This first obstacle was enough to create an anti-family attitude that would have devastated any possibility of a future healthy marriage.

Joseph was sold to Potiphar, who was the captain of Pharaoh's guard. He became Potiphar's household superintendent. Potiphar's wife attempted to seduce him, and when Joseph refused, she made a false accusation that he tried to rape her, which landed him in jail. This second obstacle would have devastated most men and further reduce the possibilities of a healthy marriage. However, Joseph rebounded and endured.

Once in jail, the warden put Joseph in charge of the other prisoners. Shortly after that, Pharaoh's cup-bearer and chief baker were thrown into the same prison. With the past betrayal by his family and Potiphar's wife, Joseph continued to help people. Joseph helped Pharaoh's cup-bearer. He predicted that the chief cup-bearer would be reinstated to his original position. However, he also predicted that the chief baker would be hanged. Joseph urged the cup-bearer to mention him to Pharaoh, but the cup-bearer did not honor his request. Once again, he was forsaken by someone who was close to him.

It was not until Pharaoh had dreams that no one else could interpret that the cup-bearer mentioned Joseph to Pharaoh. Pharaoh dreamt of seven lean cows that devoured seven fat cows as well as seven withered ears of grain that devoured seven fat ears. Pharaoh's advisers were unable to interpret the dreams. The cup-bearer remembered Joseph's talent and arranged for Joseph to interpret the dreams of Pharaoh. Joseph rose to prominence when he was able to successfully interpret the dreams of Pharaoh.

The scriptures revealed that he was a great success at saving the Egyptian people as well as his family that had abandoned him. Pharaoh arranged for Joseph to have a wife for which they had two children. While we read nothing about how he managed his family in the daily hustle and bustle of his success, the way he interacted with his family that had abandoned him provides an indication of how he interacted with his wife.

In the second year of Egyptian famine, the same brothers who had sold him into slavery were sent to Egypt to buy goods. They were sent to Joseph but did not recognize him. Joseph did recognize them and placed his brothers in prison for three days. On the third day, he brought them out of prison and requested that they return with their youngest brother, who was Joseph's immediate younger brother, to prove that they were men of good character.

After Joseph's request, his brother's spoke amongst themselves without knowing that Joseph understood Hebrew. During that discussion, his brothers were contemplating why they were treated so harshly. As Joseph listened, he has such a great emotional response that he removed himself from their presence. When he returned he imprisoned Simeon and instructed that they can only exhibit their honesty by returning with the younger brother. Joseph returned the money that they wanted to use and purchase goods along with the goods that they had requested.

During Joseph's emotional outburst, he had an opportunity to reflect on his hurts. He had the chance to reflect on all of the pain that his brothers had inflicted on him. After all of that reflection, he made a decision to do what he thought was right. He blessed them by not only providing them the goods that they desired, but he also returned the money that they used to purchase the goods. This is not the same case for many men who have faced obstacles and intend to be married or get married.

Instead, we are more likely to react to the obstacles that people have forced upon us. We will opt to respond in a manner that exacts revenge. The sad part is that we will take these same patterns into our marriage. When offended by our wives or if we feel that they have become oppositional, we will respond in a fashion that is consistent with the dysfunctional behaviors associated with our past obstacles.

- Have you ever felt that your wife is exhibiting distrustful behavior?
- How did you respond?
- Better yet, did you react or did you reflect before responding?

This is a tough position for the husband who is called to be the leader in the family. You cannot take the past feelings of distrust that are associated with past obstacles. Like Joseph, you must respond to obstacles in a manner that glorify God. This includes your responses to your wife and children.

This is the purpose of this book. Great leaders, like Joseph, have the ability to reflect on their leadership. They have an ability to reflect on their thinking and their actions before reacting to ensure a successful marriage. A man who becomes a husband must use the same process to ensure a successful marriage.

The Husband Leadership book not only helps the husband to identify those characteristics that can lead to an unsuccessful marriage, but the book guides the man through a process where he will develop a plan to overcome the atrocities associated with a dysfunctional marriage which is a product of past obstacles.

The Husband Leadership book covers five principles that overcome the characteristics related to a dysfunctional marriage. In each chapter, the husband will study the prescribed scriptures and develop a plan for overcoming each level related to a dysfunctional marriage. The Husband Leadership book is necessary because of the present difficulties that many couples have that could lead to divorce.

In the United States, it is estimated that 40%–50% of all first-time marriages will end in divorce or permanent separation. The divorce rate increases each time the person remarries. Sixty percent of those who are married for the second time end in divorce. Seventy-three percent of those who are married for the third time end in divorce.

Many researchers have cited lack of commitment as the primary contributor to divorce. Commitment helps us not to get overwhelmed by the day to day problems and challenges. When there is a high commitment in a relationship, the husband and wife feel safer and are willing to give more to the marriage to ensure it's success.

Husbands who have made a decision to remain committed will also develop a plan to ensure that the atrocities associated with any of their past obstacles will not have a negative influence on their marriage. This is the primary focus of the Husband Leadership book. The husband will develop a plan for each phase that contributes to a dysfunctional marriage.

The Husband Leadership Challenge

Likewise, ye husbands, dwell with them according to knowledge, giving honour unto the wife, as unto the weaker vessel, and as being heirs together of the grace of life; that your prayers be not hindered (1 Peter 3:7)

Many husband leadership challenges between the husband and wife result from the clash of their developed values. Values are those behaviors we learn which ultimately drive our daily actions and responses to challenging circumstances. The scriptures point out that there is only one difference in values that should lead to divorce. According to Exodus 20:14, Thou shalt not commit adultery.

When a husband and wife get married they vow that they will have a commitment to each other. They vow loyalty towards each other. The value that leads to adultery and many divorces is the lack of commitment to that vow. Or lack of loyalty.

Society teaches us that the lack of commitment or loyalty is acceptable. For example, it is acceptable to work for 5 to 7 different organizations over a lifetime. Therefore, we are taught that it is acceptable not to be loyal. Without a strong commitment to marriage many people allow societal values to dictate the outcome of our relationships.

Solomon is a biblical example of how differences in values can impact our lives. Solomon reigned over Israel for forty years. During that time he became the wealthiest man on earth, was considered one of the wisest kings, completed the construction of the temple of God, and had 1,000 wives.

But king Solomon loved many strange women, together with the daughter of Pharaoh, women of the Moabites, Ammonites, Edomites, Zidonians, and Hittites; Of the nations concerning which the Lord said unto the children of Israel, Ye shall not go in to them, neither shall they come in unto you: for surely they will turn away your heart after their gods: Solomon clave unto these in love. And he had seven hundred wives, princesses, and three hundred concubines: and his wives turned away his heart. For it came to pass, when Solomon was old, that his wives turned away his heart after other gods: and his heart was not perfect with the Lord his God, as was the heart of David his father. For Solomon went after Ashtoreth the goddess of the Zidonians, and after Milcom the abomination of the Ammonites. And Solomon did evil in the sight of the Lord, and went not fully after the Lord, as did David his father. Then did Solomon build an high place for

Chemosh, the abomination of Moab, in kthe hill that is before Jerusalem, and for Molech, the abomination of the children of Ammon (1 Kings 11: 1-7).

Solomon's wives turned him away from God and convinced him to worship and build temples to the gods that his wives supported and embraced. His wives valued different gods and this was the eventual undoing of Solomon and the Israelites (1 Kings 11:9-13).

And the LORD was angry with Solomon, because his heart was turned from the LORD God of Israel, which had appeared unto him twice, And had commanded him concerning this thing, that he should not go after other gods: but he kept not that which the LORD commanded. Wherefore the LORD said unto Solomon, Forasmuch as this is done of thee, and thou hast not kept my covenant and my statutes, which I have commanded thee, I will surely rend the kingdom from thee, and will give it to thy servant. Notwithstanding in thy days I will not do it for David thy father's sake: but I will rend it out of the hand of thy son. Howbeit I will not rend away all the kingdom; but will give one tribe to thy son for David my servant's sake, and for Jerusalem's sake which I have chosen (1 Kings 11:9-13KJV).

When the different values between a husband and wife clash the result is disunity and dysfunction within the marriage. The husband must now consider the appropriate strategy to utilize to ensure that unity remains at the center of his marriage.

The husband must first understand that the union between him and his wife form an organization. This concept is validated in scripture and secular thinking. According to Genesis 2:24 when the husband and wife are joined they become one flesh. From a scriptural standpoint they become one organization.

Therefore shall a man leave his father and his mother, and shall cleave unto his wife: and they shall be one flesh (Genesis 2:24KJV).

From a secular standpoint the husband and wife become one organization.

- Two people ➡ Organization
    - Two people become a pair
    - Pair is a couple
    - Couple is a team
    - Team is a group
    - Group is an organization

Even from a secular standpoint, when two people get married they become an organization. This is important because dysfunction organizations such as a dysfunctional marriage exhibit certain characteristics.

There are five different levels that contribute to a dysfunctional organization. Figure 1 reveals that the foundation for the dysfunctional organization begins with each person's use of *defense mechanisms* for coping. Defense mechanisms are the unwritten rules an individual learns and utilizes to effectively deal with circumstances that are upsetting, embarrassing, or threatening.

The second level is *skilled incompetence*, which is the outcome of the defense mechanisms we have internalized. When the defensive behaviors we've learned are transformed into a learned behavior, that behavior becomes a skill – albeit an incompetent skill – that we consider necessary in order to deal with issues that are embarrassing, threatening, or upsetting. A skill that is learned from the regular application of a defense mechanism has a high degree of incompetence embedded within it, because we are unaware of how this skill will impact our future.

Skilled incompetence transforms into a *defensive routine*. Defensive routines are the third level. When the skilled incompetence is automatically exhibited at all times, the behavior is now a defensive routine.

Defensive routines lead to *fancy footwork*. Fancy footwork is the fourth level. Fancy footwork happens when individuals try to deny the behavioral inconsistencies they exhibit, or else they place blame on other people, which results in distancing themselves from taking responsibility for their behavioral inconsistencies.

Fancy footwork leads to *organizational malaise*. Organizational malaise is the final level. During this phase the individuals in the organization will seek to find fault within the organization rather than accept responsibility for their actions and correct their behavior accordingly. The individual continues the process by accentuating the negative and deemphasizing the positive in an effort to cover up their actions. The organizational malaise is further exacerbated by a refusal of one or all the members to discuss their area of responsibility.

Figure 1.

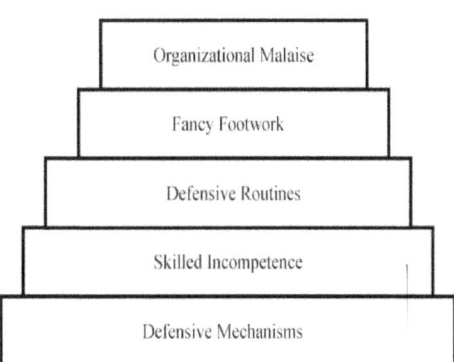

Overcoming the challenges related to a dysfunctional marriage with require that the husband embrace several leadership principles. In the next chapter, I will discuss the leadership model that will enhance the husbands ability to overcome the challenges related to a dysfunctional marriage.

The VC³S Leadership Model

My son, eat thou honey, because it is good; and the honeycomb, which is sweet to thy taste: So shall the knowledge of wisdom be unto thy soul: when thou hast found it, then there shall be a reward, and thy expectation shall not be cut off (Proverbs 24:153-14).

Leaders who are interested in overcoming the unity challenges that are presented by the behaviors of a dysfunctional organization must first begin by assessing their individual leadership behaviors. Before a leader can expect others to transition their behavior they must set the appropriate examples. Leaders who set the appropriate examples set the tone for the transition and culture of the organization. It would be hypocritical for the leader to demand certain behaviors from the members of the organization without exhibiting the desired behaviors themselves. Before the leader can talk the talk, they must walk the walk.

The book of Daniel tells us how the leader Daniel was able to walk successfully by example. The prince of the enuchs was charged with overseeing Daniel because Nebuchadnezzar, the king of Babylon, had captured Daniel and his friends and was grooming them for the kings service. In the verse Daniel 1:8, Daniel requested that the prince of eunuchs allow him to modify his diet so that he would not defile himself. Daniel did not desire to eat the king's meat or drink his wine. The prince of the enuchs feared for his life and did not want to grant Daniel's request. Daniel suggested that the prince allow him and his friends to eat the special diet for ten days. After the ten days the prince would compare them to the others that were receiving the appointed diet. Daniel could have engaged the enuch in an argument and demanded that he and his friends defer from eating the King's mandated diet. Not only would David have offended the king but he would have also created a problem for him and the prince of the enuchs. Daniels leadership is a prime example of how a leader should influence others. He also demonstrated for his friends how to use wisdom to influence others. This leadership example set the platform for the deeds that he would accomplish to glorify God.

But Daniel purposed in his heart that he would not defile himself with the portion of the king's meat, nor with the wine which he drank: therefore he requested of the prince of the eunuchs that he might not defile himself (Daniel 1:8).

Paul set a great example of great leadership too. Leaders who walk the walk must also have the determination to persevere through the good as well as the tough times. Acts 14:19-20 indicates that Paul was stoned and placed outside of the city

And there came thither certain Jews from Antioch and Iconium, who persuaded the people, and, having stoned Paul, drew him out of the city, supposing he had been dead. Howbeit, as the disciples stood round about him, he rose up, and came into the city: and the next day he departed with Barnabas to Derbe (Acts 14:19-20).

Paul's first missionary journey began at Antioch (Acts 13-14). The church in Antioch was involved in a world evangelistic mission and chose Paul and Barnabas as their representatives. After trips to several cities they decided to concentrate their efforts in the southern cities of Antioch. Typically, the missionaries would enter a town and share their message on the Sabbath day at the synagogue. Paul's message normally caused tension between believers and others who attend the synagogue. It caused so much tension that when they were at Iconium the residents that did not agree with them plotted to insult, abuse, and molest Paul and Barnabas (Acts 14:5). Paul and Barnabas departed to other local towns. While in Lystra Paul commanded a man that had never used his feet to rise up and walk. The people witnessed this and called Paul and Barnabas gods. The people wanted to offer up sacrifices for Paul and Barnabas. Paul and Barnabas convinced them they were not gods but sent to do the work of their Lord and Master - Jesus Christ. The people disobeyed them and offered up the sacrifices. Shortly, thereafter opposing Jews from Antioch arrived and persuaded and won the people to their way of thinking. They stoned Paul and dragged him to the outskirts of the town. They thought Paul was dead. The disciples surrounded Paul and Paul rose up and returned to the town. The next day Paul and Barnabas began their trip to Derbe to continue their mission of spreading the gospel of Jesus Christ of Nazareth. Daniel and Paul provide examples of leaders who set the appropriate leadership examples and then continued their path to do great things that glorified God.

Leaders must also exhibit behaviors that set the proper leadership for a dysfunctional organization. Before asking members of the organization to exhibit certain behaviors the leader must first set the example of the expected behavior. The leader must set the pattern for Godly behavior that correlates to each dysfunctional organizational behavior level. As described in chapter 1, there are five different levels that encompass a dysfunctional organization.

The Value - Character - Commitment - Communication - Self-discipline (VC^3S) Model provides a guide for leaders to follow as they set the appropriate leadership behavior for their organization. Figure 2 reveals that there are five different leadership behaviors that the leader must incorporate in their behavior before attempting to transition a dysfunctional organization.

VC³S Leadership Model

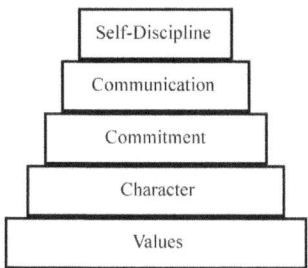

The first leadership principle that leaders must exhibit are values. Values correlate to the first dysfunctional organization level – defensive mechanisms. Like defensive mechanisms values are the significant rules that people learn from the experiences that they encounter. These rules form the basis for how people interact with other people. When these values are Christ-like then leaders have the opportunity to exhibit behaviors that are deemed acceptable to God. Leaders also have the opportunity to begin to undo the dysfunctional values that society deems as acceptable which in many cases should not be acceptable for Christian leaders who desire to transform their organization. Even more important, Christian leaders can exhibit behaviors that off-set the rules that individuals learn to ensure that they effectively deal with circumstances that are upsetting, embarrassing, or threatening.

Character is the second leadership principle that leaders must exhibit. Character correlates with the second level of a dysfunctional organization – skilled incompetence.
Skilled incompetence is developed as a result of our defensive mechanisms. Like skilled incompetence, character is developed as a result of the values that we learn. Leaders must exhibit character consistent with Christian character.

Commitment is the third leadership principle that the leader must exhibit. Skilled incompetence transforms into a defensive routines. When the skilled incompetence is automatically exhibited at all times, the behavior is now a defensive routine. A defensive routine is the same as a commitment. Unknowingly the individual becomes committed to behaviors that they developed to ensure that they avoid circumstances that are upsetting, embarrassing, or threatening. Before attempting to transition their organization, the leader must exhibit that they are committed to the God, Godly principles, the organization, and the organization members.

Communication is the fourth leadership principle that the leader must exhibit. Communication correlates to the fourth level of a dysfunctional organization – Fancy Footwork. During Fancy Footwork individuals communicate by denying that behavioral inconsistencies exist. They accomplish this by blaming others which results in them withdrawing from the circumstance. Leaders who communicate appropriately will set the proper example for people in their organization to follow.

Finally, self-discipline is the fifth leadership principle that the leader must exhibit. Self-discipline correlates to the fifth level of a dysfunctional organization. – Organizational Malaise. During this phase individuals seek to find fault with the organization rather that accepting responsibility to correct their actions. They lack the discipline to self-correct. Leaders who exhibit self-discipline characteristics have an opportunity to model for others in the organization the appropriate reactions to difficult circumstances.

In the next chapters, you will develop a leadership plan for overcoming the five levels associated with a dysfunctional organization.

Chapter 2 Scriptures

Acts 13

Now there were in the church that was at Antioch certain prophets and teachers; as Barnabas, and Simeon that was called Niger, and Lucius of Cyrene, and Manaen, which had been brought up with Herod the tetrarch, and Saul. As they ministered to the Lord, and fasted, the Holy Ghost said, Separate me Barnabas and Saul for the work whereunto I have called them. And when they had fasted and prayed, and laid their hands on them, they sent them away. So they, being sent forth by the Holy Ghost, departed unto Seleucia; and from thence they sailed to Cyprus. And when they were at Salamis, they preached the word of God in the synagogues of the Jews: and they had also John to their minister. And when they had gone through the isle unto Paphos, they found a certain sorcerer, a false prophet, a Jew, whose name was Barjesus: Which was with the deputy of the country, Sergius Paulus, a prudent man; who called for Barnabas and Saul, and desired to hear the word of God. But Elymas the sorcerer (for so is his name by interpretation) withstood them, seeking to turn away the deputy from the faith. Then Saul, (who also is called Paul,) filled with the Holy Ghost, set his eyes on him, And said, O full of all subtlety and all mischief, thou child of the devil, thou enemy of all righteousness, wilt thou not cease to pervert the right ways of the Lord? And now, behold, the hand of the Lord is upon thee, and thou shalt be blind, not seeing the sun for a season. And immediately there fell on him a mist and a darkness; and he went about seeking some to lead him by the hand. Then the deputy, when he saw what was done, believed, being astonished at the doctrine of the Lord. Now when Paul and his company loosed from Paphos, they came to Perga in Pamphylia: and John departing from them returned to Jerusalem. But when they departed from Perga, they came to Antioch in Pisidia, and went into the synagogue on the sabbath day, and sat down. And after the reading of the law and the prophets the rulers of the synagogue sent unto them, saying, Ye men and brethren, if ye have any word of exhortation for the people, say on. Then Paul stood up, and beckoning with his hand said, Men of Israel, and ye that fear God, give audience. The God of this people of Israel chose our fathers, and exalted the people when they dwelt as strangers in the land of Egypt, and with an high arm brought he them out of it. And about the time of forty years suffered he their manners in the wilderness. And when he had destroyed seven nations in the land of Chanaan, he divided their land to them by lot. And after that he gave unto them judges about the space of four hundred and fifty years, until Samuel the prophet. And afterward they desired a king: and God gave unto them Saul the son of Cis, a man of the tribe of Benjamin, by the space of forty years. And when he had removed him, he raised up unto them David to be their king; to whom also he gave testimony, and said, I have found David the son of Jesse, a man after mine own heart, which shall fulfil all my will. Of this man's seed hath God according to his promise raised unto Israel a Saviour, Jesus: When John had first preached before his coming the baptism of repentance to all the people of Israel. And as John fulfilled his course, he said, Whom think ye that I am? I am not he. But, behold, there cometh one after me, whose shoes of his feet I am not worthy to loose. Men and brethren, children of the stock of Abraham, and whosoever among you feareth God, to you is the word of this salvation sent. For they that dwell at Jerusalem, and their rulers, because they knew him not, nor yet the voices of the prophets which are read every sabbath day, they have fulfilled them in condemning him. And though they found no cause of death in him, yet desired they Pilate that he should be slain. And when they had fulfilled all that was written of him, they took him down from the tree, and laid him in a sepulchre. But God raised him from the dead: And he was seen many days of them which came up with him from Galilee to Jerusalem, who are his witnesses unto the people. And we declare unto you glad tidings, how that the promise which was made unto the fathers, God hath fulfilled the same unto us their children, in that he hath raised up Jesus again; as it is also written in the second psalm, Thou art my Son, this day have I begotten thee. And as concerning that he raised him up from the dead, now no more to return to corruption, he said on this wise, I will give you the sure mercies of David. Wherefore he saith also in another psalm, Thou shalt not suffer thine Holy One to see corruption. For David, after he had served his own generation by the will of God, fell on sleep, and was laid unto his fathers, and saw corruption: But he, whom God raised again, saw no corruption. Be it known unto you therefore, men and brethren, that through this man is preached unto you the forgiveness of sins: And by him all that believe are justified from all things, from which ye could not be justified by the law of Moses. Beware therefore, lest that come upon you, which is spoken of in the prophets; Behold, ye despisers, and wonder, and perish: for I work a work in your days, a work which ye shall in no wise believe, though a man declare it unto you. And when the Jews were gone out of the synagogue, the Gentiles besought that these words might be preached to them the next sabbath. Now when the congregation was broken up, many of the Jews and religious proselytes followed Paul and Barnabas: who, speaking to them, persuaded them to continue in the grace of God. And the next sabbath day came almost the whole city together to hear the word of God. But when the Jews saw the multitudes, they were filled with envy, and spake against those things which were spoken by Paul, contradicting and blaspheming. Then Paul and Barnabas waxed bold, and said, It was necessary that the word of God should first have been spoken to you: but seeing ye put it from you, and judge yourselves unworthy of everlasting life, lo, we turn to the Gentiles. For so hath the Lord commanded us, saying, I have set thee to be a light of the Gentiles, that thou shouldest be for salvation unto the ends of the earth. And when the Gentiles heard this, they were glad, and glorified the word of the Lord: and as many as were ordained to eternal life believed. And the word of the Lord was published throughout all the region. But the Jews stirred up the devout and honourable women, and the chief men of the city, and raised persecution against Paul and Barnabas, and expelled them out of their coasts. But they shook off the dust of their feet against them, and came unto Iconium. 52And the disciples were filled with joy, and with the Holy Ghost.

Acts 14

And it came to pass in Iconium, that they went both together into the synagogue of the Jews, and so spake, that a great multitude both of the Jews and also of the Greeks believed. But the unbelieving Jews stirred up the Gentiles, and made their minds evil affected against the brethren. Long time therefore abode they speaking boldly in the Lord, which gave testimony unto the word of his grace, and granted signs and wonders to be done by their hands. But the multitude of the city was divided: and part held with the Jews, and part with the apostles. And when there was an assault made both of the Gentiles, and also of the Jews with their rulers, to use them despitefully, and to stone them, They were ware of it, and fled unto Lystra and Derbe, cities of Lycaonia, and unto the region that lieth round about: And there they preached the gospel. And there sat a certain man at Lystra, impotent in his feet, being a cripple from his mother's womb, who never had walked: The same heard Paul speak: who stedfastly beholding him, and perceiving that he had faith to be healed, Said with a loud voice, Stand upright on thy feet. And he leaped and walked. And when the people saw what Paul had done, they lifted up their voices, saying in the speech of Lycaonia, The gods are come down to us in the likeness of men. And they called Barnabas, Jupiter; and Paul, Mercurius, because he was the chief speaker. Then the priest of Jupiter, which was before their city, brought oxen and garlands unto the gates, and would have done sacrifice with the people. Which when the apostles, Barnabas and Paul, heard of, they rent their clothes, and ran in among the people, crying out, And saying, Sirs, why do ye these things? We also are men of like passions with you, and preach unto you that ye should turn from these vanities unto the living God, which made heaven, and earth, and the sea, and all things that are therein: Who in times past suffered all nations to walk in their own ways. Nevertheless he left not himself without witness, in that he did good, and gave us rain from heaven, and fruitful seasons, filling our hearts with food and gladness. And with these sayings scarce restrained they the people, that they had not done sacrifice unto them. And there came thither certain Jews from Antioch and Iconium, who persuaded the people, and, having stoned Paul, drew him out of the city, supposing he had been dead. Howbeit, as the disciples stood round about him, he rose up, and came into the city: and the next day he departed with Barnabas to Derbe. And when they had preached the gospel to that city, and had taught many, they returned again to Lystra, and to Iconium, and Antioch, Confirming the souls of the disciples, and exhorting them to continue in the faith, and that we must through much tribulation enter into the kingdom of God. And when they had ordained them elders in every church, and had prayed with fasting, they commended them to the Lord, on whom they believed. And after they had passed throughout Pisidia, they came to Pamphylia. And when they had preached the word in Perga, they went down into Attalia: And thence sailed to Antioch, from whence they had been recommended to the grace of God for the work which they fulfilled. And when they were come, and had gathered the church together, they rehearsed all that God had done with them, and how he had opened the door of faith unto the Gentiles. And there they abode long time with the disciples.

Husband Leadership Principle #1

For a man indeed ought not to cover his head, forasmuch as he is the image and glory of God: but the woman is the glory of the man (1 Corinthians 11:7 KJV).

Husband Leadership Principle #1 involves developing Christ like values that will enhance the marriage. The values that the husband must develop and embrace are designed to overcome past experiences which would ultimately have a negative impact on his marriage.

It is important to remember that the dysfunctional marriage begins with our defensive mechanisms. Defensive mechanisms are the values that we learn from encounters and experiences that upset, embarrass, or threaten us. The husband also learns values that could have a negative impact on the survival of his marriage

In 1 Corinthians chapter 11, Paul outlines the order for marriage between the husband and wife. He emphasizes that the husband is the head of the wife and the head of the husband is God. Paul further outlines the two essential values that the husband must have. According to Paul (1 Corinthians 11:7 KJV) the two essential qualities of a man are the image of God and the glory of God.

The first husband leadership value is obedience to God's commandments. Christ is the image of God in the flesh (Colossians 1:15 - KJV) and was anointed to complete His ministry on earth (John 3:17). He was able to accomplish His ministry because of His obedience to His Father. Jesus honored His father through complete obedience (Hebrews 10:7) and followed every commandment that God gave Him as indicated by scripture.

"For I did not speak on My own initiative, but the Father Himself who sent Me has given Me commandment, what to say, and what to speak" (John 12:49).

Just as Christ's obedience to His father has bought benefits to believers, the husband's obedience to God's commandments brings benefits to him, his wife, and his family.

The second husband leadership value is to exhibit characteristics that glorify God. The Greek meaning for glory is honor, praise, and worship. To honor God requires showing respect for His authority which includes both inward emotions and outward manifestations such as gestures or actions. Praising God shows your total dependence on Him by confessing your allegiance and devotion to God. God instructs us to give Him thanks in everything (1 Thess. 5:8).

Jesus says in John 4:23-24, "But the hour is coming, and now is, when true worshippers will worship the Father in spirit and in truth, for the Father is seeking such to worship Him. God is Spirit and they that worship Him must worship Him in spirit and in truth." A true worshipper adores God. Therefore, husbands who desire to bring benefits to him, his wife, and his family must obey God's commandments and he must glorify God.

There are additional values that a husband must embrace given by God - The Father. The first set of commandments were given to us through Moses. God used Moses to deliver the Israelites from the Egyptians. After an Egyptian enslavement for over four hundred years the Israelites cried out to God and God sent Moses to deliver them. The Israelites began their journey to the Promised Land after their deliverance from the Egyptians. During that journey, God reveled to the Israelites the ten primary laws. We call these basic laws the Ten Commandments (Exodus 20: 1-17). The Ten Commandments were placed on two tablets. The first tablet focused on our relationship with God. The second tablet focused on our relationship with each other. Table 1 reveals the Old Testament Commandments in short form for each tablet.

Table 1. Old Testament Commandments – Short form

Relationship with God	*Relationship with others*
1. No gods before Me	5. Honor father and mother
2. No Idols	6. Do not murder
3. Do not take My name in vain	7. Do not commit adultery
4. Keep the Sabbath holy	8. Do not steal
	9. Do not give false testimony
	10. Do not covet

There are also additional values given by Jesus - The Son of God. A second set of commandments were given by Jesus Christ of Nazarene (Matthew 22:34-40). During His ministry He had several confrontations with the Pharisees and Sadducees. The Pharisees and Sadducees were New Testament religious and political groups that were intimidated by Jesus and sought to render His ministry fruitless. During one encounter Jesus silenced the Sadducees. The Pharisees heard about how Jesus rebuked the Sadducees. The Pharisees decided to tempt Jesus and one of their Lawyers asked Jesus "What is the great commandment in the law?" Jesus provided two basic commandments in

His response. The first is to "Love the Lord thy God with all thy heart, and with all thy soul, and with all thy mind". The second commandment is to "love thy neighbour as thyself".

But when the Pharisees had heard that he had put the Sadducees to silence, they were gathered together. Then one of them, which was a lawyer, asked him a question, tempting him, and saying, Master, which is the great commandment in the law? Jesus said unto him, Thou shalt love the Lord thy God with all thy heart, and with all thy soul, and with all thy mind. This is the first and great commandment. And the second is like unto it, Thou shalt love thy neighbour as thyself. On these two commandments hang all the law and the prophets (Matthew 22:34-40).

Each commandment is important because it is a guide to the values that husbands must follow to ensure that they are not the main factor that contributes to a dysfunctional marriage. Husbands who do not develop God centered values not only jeopardize their family but they also jeopardize their own spiritual well being.

Complete the activity which starts on the next page. This activity will help the husband to develop leadership behaviors which are consistent with the twelve commandments given by God and Jesus as well as the values outlined by the Apostle Paul. This will ensure that the husband exhibits characteristics that are consistent with the twelve primary commandments.

1.
Explain why it is important to worship no other god before God. Are there any exceptions? Write out three scriptures that support your answer.

_____

_____

_____

_____

Scripture 1:

_____

_____

Scripture 2:

_____

_____

Scripture 3:

_____

_____

_____

2.

Explain why it is important not to worship idols. Are there any exceptions? Write out three scriptures that support your answer.

___

___

___

___

___

Scripture 1:

___

___

Scripture 2:

___

___

Scripture 3:

___

___

3.
Explain why it is important not to take God's name in vain. Are there any exceptions? Write out three scriptures that support your answer.

_____
_____
_____
_____
_____

Scripture 1:

_____
_____
_____

Scripture 2:

_____
_____
_____

Scripture 3:

_____
_____
_____

4.

Explain why it is important to keep the Sabbath holy. Are there any exceptions? Write out three scriptures that support your answer.

Scripture 1:

Scripture 2:

Scripture 3:

5.
Explain why it is important to honor your father and mother. Are there any exceptions? Write out three scriptures that support your answer.

_____

_____

_____

_____

Scripture 1:

_____

_____

Scripture 2:

_____

_____

Scripture 3:

_____

_____

6.

Explain why it is important not to commit murder. Are there any exceptions? Write out three scriptures that support your answer.

_____

_____

_____

_____

_____

Scripture 1:

_____

_____

Scripture 2:

_____

_____

Scripture 3:

_____

_____

7.

Explain why it is important no to commit adultery. Are there any exceptions? Write out three scriptures that support your answer.

_____

_____

_____

_____

_____

Scripture 1:

_____

_____

Scripture 2:

_____

_____

Scripture 3:

_____

_____

8.

Explain why it is important not to steal. Are there any exceptions? Write out three scriptures that support your answer.

_____

_____

_____

_____

_____

Scripture 1:

_____

_____

Scripture 2:

_____

_____

Scripture 3:

_____

_____

9.
Explain why it is important not to give false testimony. Are there any exceptions? Write out three scriptures that support your answer.

_____

_____

_____

_____

_____

Scripture 1:

_____

_____

_____

Scripture 2:

_____

_____

_____

Scripture 3:

_____

_____

_____

10.
Explain why it is important not to covet. Are there any exceptions? Write out three scriptures that support your answer.

_____

_____

_____

_____

_____

Scripture 1:

_____

_____

Scripture 2:

_____

_____

Scripture 3:

_____

_____

Now that you have completed the activity, you will now develop on the next page a plan that will show your wife and family that you honor each principle set for by God in the Ten Commandments.

Commandment		Activity
1.	*No other gods*	
2.	*No idols*	
3.	*Do not take name in vain*	
4.	*Keep Sabbath holy*	
5.	*Honor father and mother*	
6.	*Do not murder*	
7.	*Do not commit adultery*	
8.	*Do not steal*	
9.	*Do not give false testimony*	
10.	*Do not covet*	

Next, you will complete the activity which starts on the next page. This activity will help the husband develop leadership behaviors which are consistent with the two commandments given by Jesus which are outlined in Matthew 22:34-40. .

But when the Pharisees had heard that he had put the Sadducees to silence, they were gathered together. Then one of them, which was a lawyer, asked him a question, tempting him, and saying, Master, which is the great commandment in the law? Jesus said unto him, Thou shalt love the Lord thy God with all thy heart, and with all thy soul, and with all thy mind. This is the first and great commandment. And the second is like unto it, Thou shalt love thy neighbour as thyself. On these two commandments hang all the law and the prophets (Matthew 22:34-40).

Before we begin our exercises, review the meanings of each important word outlined in Matthew 22:34-40.

Table 2.

Word	Greek Word	Greek Meaning
Love	αγαπαο	in a social or moral sense
Heart	καρδια	the thought or feelings
Soul	πσυχηε	Spirit
Mind	διανοια	Imagination
Neighbour	πλεσιον	*fellow* (Christian or friend)

11.
Explain why it is important to love the Lord thy God with all of your heart. Are there any exceptions? Provide and write out three scriptures that support your answer.

_____
_____
_____
_____
_____

Scripture 1:
_____
_____
_____

Scripture 2:
_____
_____
_____

Scripture 3:
_____
_____
_____

12a.

Explain why it is important to love the Lord thy God with all of your soul. Are there any exceptions? Provide and write out three scriptures that support your answer.

Scripture 1:

Scripture 2:

Scripture 3:

12b.

Explain why it is important to love the Lord thy God with all of your mind. Are there any exceptions? Provide and write out three scriptures that support your answer.

_____

_____

_____

_____

_____

Scripture 1:

_____

_____

_____

Scripture 2:

_____

_____

_____

Scripture 3:

_____

_____

_____

12c.
Explain why it is important to love the Lord thy neighbour. Are there any exceptions? Provide and write out three scriptures that support your answer.

_____

_____

_____

_____

_____

Scripture 1:

_____

_____

_____

Scripture 2:

_____

_____

_____

Scripture 3:

_____

_____

_____

Now that you have completed the previous activity, you will develop a plan that will show your wife and your family that you honor each principle set for by Jesus in Matthew 22:37-39.

Commandment		Activity
1a.	*Love the Lord thy God with all thy heart*	
1b.	*Love the Lord thy God with all thy soul*	
1c.	*Love the Lord thy God with all thy mind*	
2.	*Love thy neighbour as thyself*	

Now that you completed the first activity related to the first leadership value now it is time to develop values related to the second leadership value.

The second husband leadership value is to exhibit characteristics that reflect the image of God and that glorify God. According to Paul (1 Corinthians 11:7 KJV) the two essential qualities of a man are the image of God and the glory of God.

I.

Explain why it is important to exhibit characteristics that reflect the image of God. Are there any exceptions? Provide and write out three scriptures that support your answer.

_____

_____

_____

_____

_____

Scripture 1:

_____

_____

_____

Scripture 2:

_____

_____

_____

Scripture 3:

_____

_____

_____

II.
Explain why it is important to glorify God. Are there any exceptions? Provide and write out three scriptures that support your answer.

_____

_____

_____

_____

_____

Scripture 1:

_____

_____

_____

Scripture 2:

_____

_____

_____

Scripture 3:

_____

_____

_____

Now that you have completed the precious activity, you will develop a plan that will show your wife and your family that you will exhibit values consistent with the image of God and glorifying God.

Value		Activity
1.	*Image of God*	
2.	*Glory of God*	

You have completed developing activities that correlate to the defensive mechanism level of a dysfunctional marriage. The foundation for a dysfunctional marriage is the values that the husband and wife deem important. The husband is responsible for exhibiting God and Jesus centered values to begin the process for overcoming the negative foundational values of a dysfunctional marriage. The activities that you have developed embrace the twelve commandments and the importance of glorifying God. By developing the activities you will now exhibit values that are consistent with God and Christ like behavioral expectations. In the next chapter you will develop activities that are consistent with overcoming the second level for a dysfunctional marriage.

Chapter 3 Scriptures

Exodus 20:1 - 17

And God spake all these words, saying, I *am* the LORD thy God, which have brought thee out of the land of Egypt, out of the house of bondage. Thou shalt have no other gods before me. Thou shalt not make unto thee any graven image, or any likeness *of any thing* that *is* in heaven above, or that *is* in the earth beneath, or that *is* in the water under the earth: Thou shalt not bow down thyself to them, nor serve them: for I the LORD thy God *am* a jealous God, visiting the iniquity of the fathers upon the children unto the third and fourth *generation* of them that hate me; And showing mercy unto thousands of them that love me, and keep my commandments. Thou shalt not take the name of the LORD thy God in vain; for the LORD will not hold him guiltless that taketh his name in vain. Remember the sabbath day, to keep it holy. Six days shalt thou labour, and do all thy work: But the seventh day *is* the sabbath of the LORD thy God: *in it* thou shalt not do any work, thou, nor thy son, nor thy daughter, thy manservant, nor thy maidservant, nor thy cattle, nor thy stranger that *is* within thy gates: For *in* six days the LORD made heaven and earth, the sea, and all that in them *is*, and rested the seventh day: wherefore the LORD blessed the sabbath day, and hallowed it. Honour thy father and thy mother: that thy days may be long upon the land which the LORD thy God giveth thee. Thou shalt not kill. Thou shalt not commit adultery. Thou shalt not steal. Thou shalt not bear false witness against thy neighbour. Thou shalt not covet thy neighbour's house, thou shalt not covet thy neighbour's wife, nor his manservant, nor his maidservant, nor his ox, nor his ass, nor any thing that *is* thy neighbour's.

Revelation 2:1 - 7

"Unto the angel of the church of Ephesus write; These things saith he that holdeth the seven stars in his right hand, who walketh in the midst of the seven golden candlesticks; I know thy works, and thy labour, and thy patience, and how thou canst not bear them which are evil: and thou hast tried them which say they are apostles, and are not, and hast found them liars: And hast borne, and hast patience, and for my name's sake hast laboured, and hast not fainted. Nevertheless I have somewhat against thee, because thou hast left thy first love. Remember therefore from whence thou art fallen, and repent, and do the first works; or else I will come unto thee quickly, and will remove thy candlestick out of his place, except thou repent. But this thou hast, that thou hatest the deeds of the Nicolaitanes, which I also hate. He that hath an ear, let him hear what the Spirit saith unto the churches; To him that overcometh will I give to eat of the tree of life, which is in the midst of the paradise of God."

Husband Leadership Principle #2

And beside this, giving all diligence, add to your faith virtue; and to virtue knowledge; And to knowledge temperance; and to temperance patience; and to patience godliness; And to godliness brotherly kindness; and to brotherly kindness charity. For if these things be in you, and abound, they make you that ye shall neither be barren nor unfruitful in the knowledge of our Lord Jesus Christ (2 Peter 1:5-8 KJV).

The second husband leadership principle involves developing character that is consistent with obedience to God's commandments and that glorify God. Paul communicates the importance of developing character in the book of Philippians (Philippians 4:8-9 KJV). Paul states that when the appropriate character is developed that we can expect for God to be with us (Philippians 4:8-9 KJV). There is no greater feeling than knowing that God is with you in your marriage.

Finally, brethren, whatsoever things are true, whatsoever things are honest, whatsoever things are just, whatsoever things are pure, whatsoever things are lovely, whatsoever things are of good report; if there be any virtue, and if there be any praise, think on these things. Those things, which ye have both learned, and received, and heard, and seen in me, do: and the God of peace shall be with you (Philippians 4:8-9 KJV).

Paul mentions truth as the primary factor because it is mentioned first. Acquiring the truth will require wisdom and knowledge of developing character consistent with obedience to God's commandments and glorifying God.

Husbands who exhibit character that is not focused on the twelve commandments or who do not glorify God could ensure that their marriage becomes a disaster for themselves and their wife. Ananias and Sapphira provide a warning for husbands who plot to circumvent God's commandments. Ananias and Sapphira had promised to sell their land to provide financial support to the Apostles. After selling the land they decided to keep some of the money for themselves. The end result was the death of Ananias and Sapphira.

Plain and simple Ananias and Sapphira violated two primary commandments set forth by God. They violated Exodus 20:15 and Exodus 20:16. They stole and lied.

But a certain man named Ananias, with Sapphira his wife, sold a possession, And kept back part of the price, his wife also being privy to it, and brought a certain part, and laid it at the apostles' feet. But Peter said, Ananias, why hath Satan filled thine heart to lie to the Holy

Ghost, and to keep back part of the price of the land? Whiles it remained, was it not thine own? and after it was sold, was it not in thine own power? why hast thou conceived this thing in thine heart? thou hast not lied unto men, but unto God. And Ananias hearing these words fell down, and gave up the ghost: and great fear came on all them that heard these things. And the young men arose, wound him up, and carried him out, and buried him. And it was about the space of three hours after, when his wife, not knowing what was done, came in. And Peter answered unto her, Tell me whether ye sold the land for so much? And she said, Yea, for so much. Then Peter said unto her, How is it that ye have agreed together to tempt the Spirit of the Lord? behold, the feet of them which have buried thy husband are at the door, and shall carry thee out. Then fell she down straightway at his feet, and yielded up the ghost: and the young men came in, and found her dead, and, carrying her forth, buried her by her husband. And great fear came upon all the church, and upon as many as heard these things (Acts 5:1-11 KJV).

In Proverbs 2:1-11, Solomon provides the process for developing character. Developing character requires wisdom and understanding from God. Proverbs 2:6 reveals that God is the author and giver of wisdom, knowledge, and understanding. God uses His words in the Holy Bible to impart His wisdom upon us. Developing character will require that we study His twelve commandments and the glory of God.

Table 3 reveals the twelve commandments which form the foundation for the values of a Christian husband. The Christian husband leader who desires to render a dysfunctional marriage functional must develop the character necessary to overcome a dysfunctional organization such as a dysfunctional marriage.

Table 3

Commandment		Scripture
1.	*No other gods*	Exodus 20:3 (KJV)
2.	*No idols*	Exodus 20:4-6 (KJV)
3.	*Do not take name in vain*	Exodus 20:7 (KJV)
4.	*Keep Sabbath holy*	Exodus 20:8-11 (KJV)
5.	*Honor father and mother*	Exodus 20:12 (KJV)
6.	*Do not murder*	Exodus 20:13 (KJV)
7.	*Do not commit adultery*	Exodus 20:14 (KJV)
8.	*Do not steal*	Exodus 20:15 (KJV)
9.	*Do not give false testimony*	Exodus 20:16 (KJV)
10.	*Do not covet*	Exodus 20:17 (KJV)
11.	*Love the Lord thy God with all thy heart, soul, and mind*	Matthew 22:37 (KJV)
12.	*Love thy neighbour as thyself*	Matthew 22:39 (KJV)

Complete the following activities to determine the character required to facilitate a process that renders a dysfunctional marriage functional.

Commandment 1:   Exodus 20:3 KJV

Book: Exodus   **Chapter:** 20   **Verse:** 3

Write the KJV verse here: _____

_____

_____

_____

_____

What are the three key words for this verse?

1. _____

2. _____

3. _____

Compare the KJV verse with the Amplified version:

_____

_____

_____

_____

Compare the KJV verse with the New American Standard version:

_____

_____

_____

_____

Compare the KJV verse with the New International version:

_____

_____

_____

_____

What are the main differences between the versions?

_____

_____

_____

_____

Are the any scriptures that are similar to the verse?

_____

_____

_____

_____

_____

Now that you have completed the verse study for the first commandment you will complete the word study for this first commandment.

Write the first key word here: _____

Greek or Hebrew form: _____

What other scriptures have the same form for this word?

_____

_____

_____

What is the Strong's number: _____

What is the definition from the Strong's concordance?

_____

_____

_____

_____

What is the importance of this word in the verse?

_____

_____

_____

_____

What is your opinion regarding the word you have studied?

_____
_____
_____
_____
_____

Write the second key word here: _____

Greek or Hebrew form: _____

What other scriptures have the same form for this word?

_____
_____
_____

What is the Strong's number? _____

What is the definition from the Strong's concordance?

_____
_____
_____
_____
_____

What is the importance of this word in the verse?

_____

_____

_____

_____

What is your opinion regarding the word you have studied?

_____

_____

_____

_____

Write the third key word here: _____

Greek or Hebrew form: _____

What other scriptures have the same form for this word?

_____

_____

_____

What is the Strong's number? _____

What is the definition from the Strong's concordance?

_____
_____
_____
_____

What is the importance of this word in the verse?

_____
_____
_____
_____

What is your opinion regarding the word you have studied?

_____
_____
_____
_____

Commandment 2:   Exodus 20:4-6 KJV

Book: Exodus   **Chapter:** 20   **Verse:** 4-6

Write the KJV verse here: _____

_____

_____

_____

_____

What are the three key words for this verse?

1. _____

2. _____

3. _____

Compare the KJV verse with the Amplified version:

_____

_____

_____

_____

Compare the KJV verse with the New American Standard version:

_____

_____

_____

_____

Compare the KJV verse with the New International version:

_____
_____
_____
_____

What are the main differences between the versions?

_____
_____
_____
_____

Are the any scriptures that are similar to the verse?

_____
_____
_____
_____

Now that you have completed the verse study for the second commandment you will complete the word study for this second commandment.

Write the first key word here: _____

Greek or Hebrew form: _____

What other scriptures have the same form for this word?

_____

_____

_____

What is the Strong's number: _____

What is the definition from the Strong's concordance?

_____

_____

_____

_____

What is the importance of this word in the verse?

_____

_____

_____

_____

What is your opinion regarding the word you have studied?

_____

_____

_____

_____

_____

Write the second key word here: _____

Greek or Hebrew form: _____

What other scriptures have the same form for this word?

_____

_____

_____

What is the Strong's number? _____

What is the definition from the Strong's concordance?

_____

_____

_____

_____

_____

What is the importance of this word in the verse?

_____

_____

_____

_____

What is your opinion regarding the word you have studied?

_____

_____

_____

_____

Write the third key word here: _____

Greek or Hebrew form: _____

What other scriptures have the same form for this word?

_____

_____

_____

What is the Strong's number? _____

What is the definition from the Strong's concordance?

_____
_____
_____
_____

What is the importance of this word in the verse?

_____
_____
_____
_____

What is your opinion regarding the word you have studied?

_____
_____
_____
_____

Commandment 3:   Exodus 20:7 KJV

Book: Exodus **Chapter:** 20 **Verse:** 7

Write the KJV verse here: _____

_____

_____

_____

_____

What are the three key words for this verse?

1. _____

2. _____

3. _____

Compare the KJV verse with the Amplified version:

_____

_____

_____

_____

Compare the KJV verse with the New American Standard version:

_____

_____

_____

_____

Compare the KJV verse with the New International version:

_____
_____
_____
_____

What are the main differences between the versions?

_____
_____
_____
_____

Are the any scriptures that are similar to the verse?

_____
_____
_____
_____
_____

Now that you have completed the verse study for the commandment you will complete the word study for this third commandment.

Write the first key word here: _____

Greek or Hebrew form: _____

What other scriptures have the same form for this word?

_____
_____
_____

What is the Strong's number: _____

What is the definition from the Strong's concordance?

_____
_____
_____
_____

What is the importance of this word in the verse?

_____
_____
_____
_____
_____

What is your opinion regarding the word you have studied?

_____

_____

_____

_____

_____

Write the second key word here: _____

Greek or Hebrew form: _____

What other scriptures have the same form for this word?

_____

_____

_____

What is the Strong's number? _____

What is the definition from the Strong's concordance?

_____

_____

_____

_____

_____

What is the importance of this word in the verse?

_____
_____
_____
_____
_____

What is your opinion regarding the word you have studied?

_____
_____
_____
_____
_____

Write the third key word here: _____

Greek or Hebrew form: _____

What other scriptures have the same form for this word?

_____
_____
_____

What is the Strong's number? _____

What is the definition from the Strong's concordance?

_____
_____
_____
_____

What is the importance of this word in the verse?

_____
_____
_____
_____

What is your opinion regarding the word you have studied?

_____
_____
_____
_____

Commandment 4:   Exodus 20:8-11 KJV

Book: Exodus   **Chapter:** 20   **Verse:** 8-11

Write the KJV verse here: _____

_____

_____

_____

_____

What are the three key words for this verse?

1. _____

2. _____

3. _____

Compare the KJV verse with the Amplified version:

_____

_____

_____

_____

Compare the KJV verse with the New American Standard version:

_____

_____

_____

_____

Compare the KJV verse with the New International version:

_____

_____

_____

_____

What are the main differences between the versions?

_____

_____

_____

_____

Are the any scriptures that are similar to the verse?

_____

_____

_____

_____

Now that you have completed the verse study for the fourth commandment you will complete the word study for this fourth commandment.

Write the first key word here: _____

Greek or Hebrew form: _____

What other scriptures have the same form for this word?

_____

_____

_____

What is the Strong's number: _____

What is the definition from the Strong's concordance?

_____

_____

_____

_____

What is the importance of this word in the verse?

_____

_____

_____

_____

What is your opinion regarding the word you have studied?

_____

_____

_____

_____

_____

Write the second key word here: _____

Greek or Hebrew form: _____

What other scriptures have the same form for this word?

_____

_____

_____

What is the Strong's number? _____

What is the definition from the Strong's concordance?

_____

_____

_____

_____

What is the importance of this word in the verse?

_____

_____

_____

_____

_____

What is your opinion regarding the word you have studied?

_____

_____

_____

_____

_____

Write the third key word here: _____

Greek or Hebrew form: _____

What other scriptures have the same form for this word?

_____

_____

_____

What is the Strong's number? _____

What is the definition from the Strong's concordance?

_____
_____
_____
_____

What is the importance of this word in the verse?

_____
_____
_____
_____

What is your opinion regarding the word you have studied?

_____
_____
_____
_____

Commandment 5:   Exodus 20:12 KJV

Book: Exodus   **Chapter:** 20   **Verse:** 12

Write the KJV verse here:

_____

_____

_____

_____

_____

What are the three key words for this verse?

1. _____

2. _____

3. _____

Compare the KJV verse with the Amplified version:

_____

_____

_____

_____

Compare the KJV verse with the New American Standard version:

_____

_____

_____

_____

Compare the KJV verse with the New International version:

_____
_____
_____
_____

What are the main differences between the versions?

_____
_____
_____
_____

Are the any scriptures that are similar to the verse?

_____
_____
_____
_____
_____

Now that you have completed the verse study for the commandment you will complete the word study for this fifth commandment.

Write the first key word here: _____

Greek or Hebrew form: _____

What other scriptures have the same form for this word?

_____

_____

_____

What is the Strong's number: _____

What is the definition from the Strong's concordance?

_____

_____

_____

_____

What is the importance of this word in the verse?

_____

_____

_____

_____

What is your opinion regarding the word you have studied?

_____

_____

_____

_____

_____

Write the second key word here: _____

Greek or Hebrew form: _____

What other scriptures have the same form for this word?

_____

_____

_____

What is the Strong's number? _____

What is the definition from the Strong's concordance?

_____

_____

_____

_____

_____

What is the importance of this word in the verse?

_____

_____

_____

_____

_____

What is your opinion regarding the word you have studied?

_____

_____

_____

_____

_____

Write the third key word here: _____

Greek or Hebrew form: _____

What other scriptures have the same form for this word?

_____

_____

_____

What is the Strong's number? _____

What is the definition from the Strong's concordance?

_____

_____

_____

_____

What is the importance of this word in the verse?

_____

_____

_____

_____

What is your opinion regarding the word you have studied?

_____

_____

_____

_____

Commandment 6:   Exodus 20:12 KJV

Book: Exodus   **Chapter:** 20   **Verse:** 12

Write the KJV verse here: _____

_____

_____

_____

_____

What are the three key words for this verse?

1. _____

2. _____

3. _____

Compare the KJV verse with the Amplified version:

_____

_____

_____

_____

Compare the KJV verse with the New American Standard version:

_____

_____

_____

_____

Compare the KJV verse with the New International version:

_____

_____

_____

_____

What are the main differences between the versions?

_____

_____

_____

_____

Are the any scriptures that are similar to the verse?

_____

_____

_____

_____

Now that you have completed the verse study for the commandment you will complete the word study for this sixth commandment.

Write the first key word here: _____

Greek or Hebrew form: _____

What other scriptures have the same form for this word?

_____

_____

_____

What is the Strong's number: _____

What is the definition from the Strong's concordance?

_____

_____

_____

_____

What is the importance of this word in the verse?

_____

_____

_____

_____

_____

What is your opinion regarding the word you have studied?

_____

_____

_____

_____

_____

Write the second key word here: _____

Greek or Hebrew form: _____

What other scriptures have the same form for this word?

_____

_____

_____

What is the Strong's number? _____

What is the definition from the Strong's concordance?

_____

_____

_____

_____

_____

What is the importance of this word in the verse?

_____
_____
_____
_____
_____

What is your opinion regarding the word you have studied?

_____
_____
_____
_____
_____

Write the third key word here: _____

Greek or Hebrew form: _____

What other scriptures have the same form for this word?

_____
_____
_____

What is the Strong's number? _____

What is the definition from the Strong's concordance?

_____
_____
_____
_____

What is the importance of this word in the verse?

_____
_____
_____
_____

What is your opinion regarding the word you have studied?

_____
_____
_____
_____

Commandment 7:   Exodus 20:14 KJV

Book: Exodus   **Chapter:** 20   **Verse:** 14

Write the KJV verse here: _____

_____

_____

_____

_____

What are the three key words for this verse?

1. _____

2. _____

3. _____

Compare the KJV verse with the Amplified version:

_____

_____

_____

_____

Compare the KJV verse with the New American Standard version:

_____

_____

_____

_____

Compare the KJV verse with the New International version:

_____
_____
_____
_____

What are the main differences between the versions?

_____
_____
_____
_____

Are the any scriptures that are similar to the verse?

_____
_____
_____
_____
_____

Now that you have completed the verse study for the commandment you will complete the word study for this seventh commandment.

Write the first key word here: _____

Greek or Hebrew form: _____

What other scriptures have the same form for this word?

_____

_____

_____

What is the Strong's number: _____

What is the definition from the Strong's concordance?

_____

_____

_____

_____

What is the importance of this word in the verse?

_____

_____

_____

_____

What is your opinion regarding the word you have studied?

_____

_____

_____

_____

_____

Write the second key word here: _____

Greek or Hebrew form: _____

What other scriptures have the same form for this word?

_____

_____

_____

What is the Strong's number? _____

What is the definition from the Strong's concordance?

_____

_____

_____

_____

What is the importance of this word in the verse?

_____

_____

_____

_____

_____

What is your opinion regarding the word you have studied?

_____

_____

_____

_____

_____

Write the third key word here: _____

Greek or Hebrew form: _____

What other scriptures have the same form for this word?

_____

_____

_____

What is the Strong's number? _____

What is the definition from the Strong's concordance?

_____
_____
_____
_____
_____

What is the importance of this word in the verse?

_____
_____
_____
_____
_____

What is your opinion regarding the word you have studied?

_____
_____
_____
_____
_____

Commandment 8:   Exodus 20:15 KJV

Book: Exodus   **Chapter:** 20   **Verse:** 15

Write the KJV verse here: _____

_____

_____

_____

_____

What are the three key words for this verse?

1. _____

2. _____

3. _____

Compare the KJV verse with the Amplified version:

_____

_____

_____

_____

Compare the KJV verse with the New American Standard version:

_____

_____

_____

_____

Compare the KJV verse with the New International version:

_____

_____

_____

_____

What are the main differences between the versions?

_____

_____

_____

_____

Are the any scriptures that are similar to the verse?

_____

_____

_____

_____

_____

Now that you have completed the verse study for the commandment you will complete the word study for this eighth commandment.

Write the first key word here: _____

Greek or Hebrew form: _____

What other scriptures have the same form for this word?

_____

_____

_____

What is the Strong's number: _____

What is the definition from the Strong's concordance?

_____

_____

_____

_____

What is the importance of this word in the verse?

_____

_____

_____

_____

What is your opinion regarding the word you have studied?

_____
_____
_____
_____
_____

Write the second key word here: _____

Greek or Hebrew form: _____

What other scriptures have the same form for this word?

_____
_____
_____

What is the Strong's number? _____

What is the definition from the Strong's concordance?

_____
_____
_____
_____
_____

What is the importance of this word in the verse?

_____
_____
_____
_____
_____

What is your opinion regarding the word you have studied?

_____
_____
_____
_____
_____

Write the third key word here: _____

Greek or Hebrew form: _____

What other scriptures have the same form for this word?

_____
_____
_____

What is the Strong's number? _____

What is the definition from the Strong's concordance?

_____
_____
_____
_____
_____

What is the importance of this word in the verse?

_____
_____
_____
_____
_____

What is your opinion regarding the word you have studied?

_____
_____
_____
_____
_____

Commandment 9:   Exodus 20:16 KJV

Book: Exodus **Chapter:** 20 **Verse:** 3

Write the KJV verse here: _____

_____

_____

_____

_____

What are the three key words for this verse?

1. _____

2. _____

3. _____

Compare the KJV verse with the Amplified version:

_____

_____

_____

_____

Compare the KJV verse with the New American Standard version:

_____

_____

_____

_____

Compare the KJV verse with the New International version:

_____
_____
_____
_____

What are the main differences between the versions?

_____
_____
_____
_____

Are the any scriptures that are similar to the verse?

_____
_____
_____
_____
_____

Now that you have completed the verse study for the commandment you will complete the word study for this ninth commandment.

Write the first key word here: _____

Greek or Hebrew form: _____

What other scriptures have the same form for this word?

_____

_____

_____

What is the Strong's number: _____

What is the definition from the Strong's concordance?

_____

_____

_____

_____

What is the importance of this word in the verse?

_____

_____

_____

_____

_____

What is your opinion regarding the word you have studied?

_____

_____

_____

_____

_____

Write the second key word here: _____

Greek or Hebrew form: _____

What other scriptures have the same form for this word?

_____

_____

_____

What is the Strong's number? _____

What is the definition from the Strong's concordance?

_____

_____

_____

_____

_____

What is the importance of this word in the verse?

_____

_____

_____

_____

_____

What is your opinion regarding the word you have studied?

_____

_____

_____

_____

_____

Write the third key word here: _____

Greek or Hebrew form: _____

What other scriptures have the same form for this word?

_____

_____

_____

What is the Strong's number? _____

What is the definition from the Strong's concordance?
_____
_____
_____
_____

What is the importance of this word in the verse?
_____
_____
_____
_____

What is your opinion regarding the word you have studied?
_____
_____
_____
_____

Commandment 10:   Exodus 20:17 KJV

Book: Exodus   **Chapter:** 20   **Verse:** 17

Write the KJV verse here: _____

_____

_____

_____

_____

What are the three key words for this verse?

1. _____

2. _____

3. _____

Compare the KJV verse with the Amplified version:

_____

_____

_____

Compare the KJV verse with the New American Standard version:

_____

_____

_____

_____

Compare the KJV verse with the New International version:

_____

_____

_____

_____

What are the main differences between the versions?

_____

_____

_____

_____

Are the any scriptures that are similar to the verse?

_____

_____

_____

_____

Now that you have completed the verse study for the commandment you will complete the word study for this tenth commandment.

Write the first key word here: _____

Greek or Hebrew form: _____

What other scriptures have the same form for this word?

_____
_____
_____

What is the Strong's number: _____

What is the definition from the Strong's concordance?

_____
_____
_____
_____

What is the importance of this word in the verse?

_____
_____
_____
_____

What is your opinion regarding the word you have studied?

_____
_____
_____
_____
_____

Write the second key word here: _____

Greek or Hebrew form: _____

What other scriptures have the same form for this word?

_____
_____
_____

What is the Strong's number? _____

What is the definition from the Strong's concordance?

_____
_____
_____
_____
_____

What is the importance of this word in the verse?

_____
_____
_____
_____
_____

What is your opinion regarding the word you have studied?

_____
_____
_____
_____
_____

Write the third key word here: _____

Greek or Hebrew form: _____

What other scriptures have the same form for this word?

_____
_____
_____

What is the Strong's number? _____

What is the definition from the Strong's concordance?

_____
_____
_____
_____
_____

What is the importance of this word in the verse?

_____
_____
_____
_____
_____

What is your opinion regarding the word you have studied?

_____
_____
_____
_____
_____

Commandment 11:   Matthew 22:37 KJV

Book: Matthew **Chapter:** 22 **Verse:** 37

Write the KJV verse here: _____

_____

_____

_____

_____

What are the three key words for this verse?

1. _____

2. _____

3. _____

Compare the KJV verse with the Amplified version:

_____

_____

_____

_____

Compare the KJV verse with the New American Standard version:

_____

_____

_____

_____

Compare the KJV verse with the New International version:

_____

_____

_____

_____

What are the main differences between the versions?

_____

_____

_____

_____

Are the any scriptures that are similar to the verse?

_____

_____

_____

_____

Now that you have completed the verse study for the commandment you will complete the word study for this eleventh commandment.

Write the first key word here: _____

Greek or Hebrew form: _____

What other scriptures have the same form for this word?

_____
_____
_____

What is the Strong's number: _____

What is the definition from the Strong's concordance?

_____
_____
_____
_____
_____

What is the importance of this word in the verse?

_____
_____
_____
_____
_____

What is your opinion regarding the word you have studied?

_____

_____

_____

_____

_____

Write the second key word here: _____

Greek or Hebrew form: _____

What other scriptures have the same form for this word?

_____

_____

_____

What is the Strong's number? _____

What is the definition from the Strong's concordance?

_____

_____

_____

_____

_____

What is the importance of this word in the verse?

_____

_____

_____

_____

_____

What is your opinion regarding the word you have studied?

_____

_____

_____

_____

_____

Write the third key word here: _____

Greek or Hebrew form: _____

What other scriptures have the same form for this word?

_____

_____

_____

What is the Strong's number? _____

What is the definition from the Strong's concordance?

_____

_____

_____

_____

What is the importance of this word in the verse?

_____

_____

_____

_____

What is your opinion regarding the word you have studied?

_____

_____

_____

_____

Commandment 12:   Matthew 22:39 KJV

Book: Matthew **Chapter:** 22 **Verse:** 39

Write the KJV verse here: _____

_____

_____

_____

_____

What are the three key words for this verse?

1. _____

2. _____

3. _____

Compare the KJV verse with the Amplified version:

_____

_____

_____

_____

Compare the KJV verse with the New American Standard version:

_____

_____

_____

_____

Compare the KJV verse with the New International version:

_____

_____

_____

_____

What are the main differences between the versions?

_____

_____

_____

_____

Are the any scriptures that are similar to the verse?

_____

_____

_____

_____

Now that you have completed the verse study for the commandment you will complete the word study for this twelfth commandment.

Write the first key word here: _____

Greek or Hebrew form: _____

What other scriptures have the same form for this word?

_____

_____

_____

What is the Strong's number: _____

What is the definition from the Strong's concordance?

_____

_____

_____

_____

What is the importance of this word in the verse?

_____

_____

_____

_____

What is your opinion regarding the word you have studied?

_____
_____
_____
_____
_____

Write the second key word here: _____

Greek or Hebrew form: _____

What other scriptures have the same form for this word?

_____
_____
_____

What is the Strong's number? _____

What is the definition from the Strong's concordance?

_____
_____
_____
_____
_____

What is the importance of this word in the verse?

_____

_____

_____

_____

What is your opinion regarding the word you have studied?

_____

_____

_____

_____

Write the third key word here: _____

Greek or Hebrew form: _____

What other scriptures have the same form for this word?

_____

_____

_____

What is the Strong's number? _____

What is the definition from the Strong's concordance?

_____

_____

_____

_____

What is the importance of this word in the verse?

_____

_____

_____

_____

What is your opinion regarding the word you have studied?

_____

_____

_____

_____

The second husband leadership value is to exhibit characteristics that glorify God. The Greek meaning for glory is honor, praise, and worship. Proverbs 3:9, 2 Chronicles 20:21, and 1 John 4:23-24 provide instructions on how to honor, praise, and worship God respectively.

Glorify 1: Proverbs 3:9 KJV

Book: Proverbs **Chapter:** 3 **Verse:** 9

Write the KJV verse here: _____

_____

_____

_____

_____

What are the three key words for this verse?

1. _____

2. _____

3. _____

Compare the KJV verse with the Amplified version:

_____

_____

_____

_____

Compare the KJV verse with the New American Standard version:

_____

_____

_____

_____

Compare the KJV verse with the New International version:

_____
_____
_____
_____

What are the main differences between the versions?

_____
_____
_____
_____

Are the any scriptures that are similar to the verse?

_____
_____
_____
_____
_____

Now that you have completed the verse study for the commandment you will complete the word study for this commandment.

Write the first key word here: _____

Greek or Hebrew form: _____

What other scriptures have the same form for this word?

_____

_____

_____

What is the Strong's number: _____

What is the definition from the Strong's concordance?

_____

_____

_____

_____

What is the importance of this word in the verse?

_____

_____

_____

_____

_____

What is your opinion regarding the word you have studied?

_____

_____

_____

_____

_____

Write the second key word here: _____

Greek or Hebrew form: _____

What other scriptures have the same form for this word?

_____

_____

_____

What is the Strong's number? _____

What is the definition from the Strong's concordance?

_____

_____

_____

_____

_____

What is the importance of this word in the verse?

_____

_____

_____

_____

_____

What is your opinion regarding the word you have studied?

_____

_____

_____

_____

Write the third key word here: _____

Greek or Hebrew form: _____

What other scriptures have the same form for this word?

_____

_____

_____

What is the Strong's number? _____

What is the definition from the Strong's concordance?

_____

_____

_____

_____

_____

What is the importance of this word in the verse?

_____

_____

_____

_____

_____

What is your opinion regarding the word you have studied?

_____

_____

_____

_____

_____

Glorify 2:   2 Chronicles 20:21 KJV

Book: 2 Chronicles   **Chapter:** 20   **Verse:** 21

Write the KJV verse here: _____

_____

_____

_____

_____

What are the three key words for this verse?

1. _____

2. _____

3. _____

Compare the KJV verse with the Amplified version:

_____

_____

_____

_____

Compare the KJV verse with the New American Standard version:

_____

_____

_____

_____

Compare the KJV verse with the New International version:

_____
_____
_____
_____

What are the main differences between the versions?

_____
_____
_____
_____

Are the any scriptures that are similar to the verse?

_____
_____
_____
_____

Now that you have completed the verse study for the commandment you will complete the word study for this commandment.

Write the first key word here: _____

Greek or Hebrew form: _____

What other scriptures have the same form for this word?

_____

_____

_____

What is the Strong's number? _____

What is the definition from the Strong's concordance?

_____

_____

_____

_____

What is the importance of this word in the verse?

_____

_____

_____

_____

What is your opinion regarding the word you have studied?

_____

_____

_____

_____

_____

Write the second key word here: _____

Greek or Hebrew form: _____

What other scriptures have the same form for this word?

_____

_____

_____

What is the Strong's number? _____

What is the definition from the Strong's concordance?

_____

_____

_____

_____

_____

What is the importance of this word in the verse?

_____
_____
_____
_____
_____

What is your opinion regarding the word you have studied?

_____
_____
_____
_____
_____

Write the third key word here: _____

Greek or Hebrew form: _____

What other scriptures have the same form for this word?

_____
_____
_____

What is the Strong's number? _____

What is the definition from the Strong's concordance?

_____
_____
_____
_____
_____

What is the importance of this word in the verse?

_____
_____
_____
_____
_____

What is your opinion regarding the word you have studied?

_____
_____
_____
_____
_____

Glorify 3A: John 4:23 KJV

Book: John   **Chapter:** 4   **Verse:** 23

Write the KJV verse here: _____

_____

_____

_____

_____

What are the three key words for this verse?

1. _____

2. _____

3. _____

Compare the KJV verse with the Amplified version:

_____

_____

_____

_____

Compare the KJV verse with the New American Standard version:

_____

_____

_____

_____

Compare the KJV verse with the New International version:

_____
_____
_____
_____

What are the main differences between the versions?

_____
_____
_____
_____

Are the any scriptures that are similar to the verse?

_____
_____
_____
_____
_____

Now that you have completed the verse study for the commandment you will complete the word study for this commandment.

Write the first key word here: _____

Greek or Hebrew form: _____

What other scriptures have the same form for this word?

_____

_____

_____

What is the Strong's number: _____

What is the definition from the Strong's concordance?

_____

_____

_____

_____

What is the importance of this word in the verse?

_____

_____

_____

_____

_____

What is your opinion regarding the word you have studied?

_____

_____

_____

_____

_____

Write the second key word here: _____

Greek or Hebrew form: _____

What other scriptures have the same form for this word?

_____

_____

_____

What is the Strong's number? _____

What is the definition from the Strong's concordance?

_____

_____

_____

_____

_____

What is the importance of this word in the verse?

_____

_____

_____

_____

_____

What is your opinion regarding the word you have studied?

_____

_____

_____

_____

Write the third key word here: _____

Greek or Hebrew form: _____

What other scriptures have the same form for this word?

_____

_____

_____

What is the Strong's number? _____

What is the definition from the Strong's concordance?

_____

_____

_____

_____

_____

What is the importance of this word in the verse?

_____

_____

_____

_____

_____

What is your opinion regarding the word you have studied?

_____

_____

_____

_____

_____

Glorify 3B: John 4:24 KJV

Book: John   **Chapter:** 4   **Verse:** 23

Write the KJV verse here: _____

_____

_____

_____

_____

What are the three key words for this verse?

1. _____

2. _____

3. _____

Compare the KJV verse with the Amplified version:

_____

_____

_____

_____

Compare the KJV verse with the New American Standard version:

_____

_____

_____

_____

Compare the KJV verse with the New International version:

_____

_____

_____

_____

What are the main differences between the versions?

_____

_____

_____

_____

Are the any scriptures that are similar to the verse?

_____

_____

_____

_____

_____

Now that you have completed the verse study for the commandment you will complete the word study for this commandment.

Write the first key word here: _____

Greek or Hebrew form: _____

What other scriptures have the same form for this word?

_____
_____
_____

What is the Strong's number? _____

What is the definition from the Strong's concordance?

_____
_____
_____
_____

What is the importance of this word in the verse?

_____
_____
_____
_____

What is your opinion regarding the word you have studied?

_____

_____

_____

_____

_____

Write the second key word here: _____

Greek or Hebrew form: _____

What other scriptures have the same form for this word?

_____

_____

_____

What is the Strong's number? _____

What is the definition from the Strong's concordance?

_____

_____

_____

_____

_____

What is the importance of this word in the verse?

_____

_____

_____

_____

What is your opinion regarding the word you have studied?

_____

_____

_____

_____

Write the third key word here: _____

Greek or Hebrew form: _____

What other scriptures have the same form for this word?

_____

_____

_____

What is the Strong's number? _____

What is the definition from the Strong's concordance?

_____

_____

_____

_____

What is the importance of this word in the verse?

_____

_____

_____

_____

What is your opinion regarding the word you have studied?

_____

_____

_____

_____

You have completed developing activities that correlate to the skilled incompetence level. The activities that you have developed embrace the twelve commandments outlined in the Old and New Testament. By developing the activities you will now exhibit character behavior that is consistent with the image and glory of God. In the next chapter you will develop activities that are consistent with the commitment level.

Chapter 4 Scriptures

Judges 9:22 – 57

When Abimelech had reigned three years over Israel, Then God sent an evil spirit between Abimelech and the men of Shechem; and the men of Shechem dealt treacherously with Abimelech: That the cruelty *done* to the threescore and ten sons of Jerubbaal might come, and their blood be laid upon Abimelech their brother, which slew them; and upon the men of Shechem, which aided him in the killing of his brethren. And the men of Shechem set liers in wait for him in the top of the mountains, and they robbed all that came along that way by them: and it was told Abimelech. And Gaal the son of Ebed came with his brethren, and went over to Shechem: and the men of Shechem put their confidence in him. And they went out into the fields, and gathered their vineyards, and trode *the grapes*, and made merry, and went into the house of their god, and did eat and drink, and cursed Abimelech. And Gaal the son of Ebed said, Who *is* Abimelech, and who *is* Shechem, that we should serve him? *is* not *he* the son of Jerubbaal? and Zebul his officer? serve the men of Hamor the father of Shechem: for why should we serve him? And would to God this people were under my hand! then would I remove Abimelech. And he said to Abimelech, Increase thine army, and come out. And when Zebul the ruler of the city heard the words of Gaal the son of Ebed, his anger was kindled. And he sent messengers unto Abimelech privily, saying, Behold, Gaal the son of Ebed and his brethren be come to Shechem; and, behold, they fortify the city against thee. Now therefore up by night, thou and the people that *is* with thee, and lie in wait in the field: And it shall be, *that* in the morning, as soon as the sun is up, thou shalt rise early, and set upon the city: and, behold, *when* he and the people that *is* with him come out against thee, then mayest thou do to them as thou shalt find occasion. And Abimelech rose up, and all the people that *were* with him, by night, and they laid wait against Shechem in four companies. And Gaal the son of Ebed went out, and stood in the entering of the gate of the city: and Abimelech rose up, and the people that *were* with him, from lying in wait. And when Gaal saw the people, he said to Zebul, Behold, there come people down from the top of the mountains. And Zebul said unto him, Thou seest the shadow of the mountains as *if they were* men. And Gaal spake again and said, See there come people down by the middle of the land, and another company come along by the plain of Meonenim. Then said Zebul unto him, Where *is* now thy mouth, wherewith thou saidst, Who *is* Abimelech, that we should serve him? *is* not this the people that thou hast despised? go out, I pray now, and fight with them. And Gaal went out before the men of Shechem, and fought with Abimelech. And Abimelech chased him, and he fled before him, and many were overthrown *and* wounded, *even* unto the entering of the gate. And Abimelech dwelt at Arumah: and Zebul thrust out Gaal and his brethren, that they should not dwell in Shechem. And it came to pass on the morrow, that the people went out into the field; and they told Abimelech. And he took the people, and divided them into three companies, and laid wait in the field, and looked, and, behold, the people *were* come forth out of the city; and he rose up against them, and smote them. And Abimelech, and the company that *was* with him, rushed forward, and stood in the entering of the gate of the city: and the two *other* companies ran upon all *the people* that *were* in the fields, and slew them. And Abimelech fought against the city all that day;

and he took the city, and slew the people that *was* therein, and beat down the city, and sowed it with salt. And when all the men of the tower of Shechem heard *that*, they entered into an hold of the house of the god Berith. And it was told Abimelech, that all the men of the tower of Shechem were gathered together. And Abimelech gat him up to mount Zalmon, he and all the people that *were* with him; and Abimelech took an axe in his hand, and cut down a bough from the trees, and took it, and laid *it* on his shoulder, and said unto the people that *were* with him, What ye have seen me do, make haste, *and* do as I *have done*. And all the people likewise cut down every man his bough, and followed Abimelech, and put *them* to the hold, and set the hold on fire upon them; so that all the men of the tower of Shechem died also, about a thousand men and women. Then went Abimelech to Thebez, and encamped against Thebez, and took it. But there was a strong tower within the city, and thither fled all the men and women, and all they of the city, and shut *it* to them, and gat them up to the top of the tower. And Abimelech came unto the tower, and fought against it, and went hard unto the door of the tower to burn it with fire. And a certain woman cast a piece of a millstone upon Abimelech's head, and all to brake his skull. Then he called hastily unto the young man his armourbearer, and said unto him, Draw thy sword, and slay me, that men say not of me, A woman slew him. And his young man thrust him through, and he died. And when the men of Israel saw that Abimelech was dead, they departed every man unto his place. Thus God rendered the wickedness of Abimelech, which he did unto his father, in slaying his seventy brethren: And all the evil of the men of Shechem did God render upon their heads: and upon them came the curse of Jotham the son of Jerubbaal.

Proverbs 2:1 – 11

My son, if thou wilt receive my words, and hide my commandments with thee; So that thou incline thine ear unto wisdom, *and* apply thine heart to understanding; Yea, if thou criest after knowledge, *and* liftest up thy voice for understanding; If thou seekest her as silver, and searchest for her as *for* hid treasures; Then shalt thou understand the fear of the LORD, and find the knowledge of God. For the LORD giveth wisdom: out of his mouth *cometh* knowledge and understanding. He layeth up sound wisdom for the righteous: *he is* a buckler to them that walk uprightly. He keepeth the paths of judgment, and preserveth the way of his saints. Then shalt thou understand righteousness, and judgment, and equity; *yea*, every good path. When wisdom entereth into thine heart, and knowledge is pleasant unto thy soul; Discretion shall preserve thee, understanding shall keep thee:

Husband Leadership Principle # 3

I beseech you therefore, brethren, by the mercies of God, that ye present your bodies a living sacrifice, holy, acceptable unto God, which is your reasonable service. And be not conformed to this world: but be ye transformed by the renewing of your mind, that ye may prove what is that good, and acceptable, and perfect, will of God (Romans 12:1-2KJV).

Commitment is the third leadership behavior that husbands must exhibit. Commitment is the counterbalance to defensive routines. Defensive routines are the behaviors that become automatic as a result of skilled incompetence and contribute to the dysfunctional marriage. Husbands who develop a commitment to the image of God and glorifying God will exhibit behaviors that counterbalance the defensive routines of a dysfunctional marriage.

Commitment is an important characteristic that God possesses. God showed His commitment to the Jews in Jeremiah 31:31-36. Jeremiah was a great prophet of God who assisted King Josiah in his quest to reform Israel (2 Kings 23:1-25). King Josiah made a commitment to glorify God which resulted in the people making the same commitment (2 Kings 23:3).

And the king stood by a pillar, and made a covenant before the LORD, to walk after the LORD, and to keep his commandments and his testimonies and his statutes with all their heart and all their soul, to perform the words of this covenant that were written in this book. And all the people stood to the covenant (2 Kings 23:3 KJV).

Effective leadership requires that the husband sincerely commit their lives to God. In Romans 12:1-2 Paul urges us to devote ourselves completely to God.

I beseech you therefore, brethren, by the mercies of God, that ye present your bodies a living sacrifice, holy, acceptable unto God, which is your reasonable service. And be not conformed to this world: but be ye transformed by the renewing of your mind, that ye may prove what is that good, and acceptable, and perfect, will of God (Romans 12:1 – 2).

During this phase of the transformation the husband must exhibit behavior that is consistent with the image and glory of God too. In this chapter you will respond to how you would apply the image and glory of God to your personal life and to your marriage.

Complete the activity that follows to continue the development of leadership principles that enhance a husband's leadership.

Commandment 1:   Exodus 20:3 KJV

Explain why commandment 1 is important.

How will you apply this verse to your personal life?

How will you apply this verse to your relationship with your wife?

Commandment 2:   Exodus 20:4-6 KJV

Explain why commandment 2 is important.

_____
_____
_____
_____
_____
_____

How will you apply this verse to your personal life?

_____
_____
_____
_____
_____
_____

How will you apply this verse to your relationship with your wife?

_____
_____
_____
_____
_____
_____

Commandment 3:   Exodus 20:7 KJV

Explain why commandment 3 is important.

How will you apply this verse to your personal life?

How will you apply this verse to your relationship with your wife?

Commandment 4:   Exodus 20:8-11 KJV

Explain why commandment 4 is important.

_____

How will you apply this verse to your personal life?

_____

How will you apply this verse to your relationship with your wife?

_____

Commandment 5:   Exodus 20:12 KJV

Explain why commandment 5 is important.

How will you apply this verse to your personal life?

How will you apply this verse to your relationship with your wife?

Commandment 6:   Exodus 20:13 KJV

Explain why commandment 6 is important.

_____
_____
_____
_____
_____
_____

How will you apply this verse to your personal life?

_____
_____
_____
_____
_____
_____

How will you apply this verse to your relationship with your wife?

_____
_____
_____
_____
_____
_____

Commandment 7:   Exodus 20:14 KJV

Explain why commandment 7 is important.

How will you apply this verse to your personal life?

How will you apply this verse to your relationship with your wife?

Commandment 8: Exodus 20:15 KJV

Explain why commandment 8 is important.

_____
_____
_____
_____
_____
_____

How will you apply this verse to your personal life?

_____
_____
_____
_____
_____
_____

How will you apply this verse to your relationship with your wife?

_____
_____
_____
_____
_____
_____

Commandment 9:   Exodus 20:16 KJV

Explain why commandment 9 is important.

_____

_____

_____

_____

_____

_____

How will you apply this verse to your personal life?

_____

_____

_____

_____

_____

_____

How will you apply this verse to your relationship with your wife?

_____

_____

_____

_____

_____

_____

Commandment 10:   Exodus 20:17 KJV

Explain why commandment 10 is important.

_____

_____

_____

_____

_____

_____

How will you apply this verse to your personal life?

_____

_____

_____

_____

_____

_____

How will you apply this verse to your relationship with your wife?

_____

_____

_____

_____

_____

_____

Commandment 11:   Matthew 22:37 (KJV)

Explain why commandment 11 is important.

_____

_____

_____

_____

_____

_____

How will you apply this verse to your personal life?

_____

_____

_____

_____

_____

How will you apply this verse to your relationship with your wife?

_____

_____

_____

_____

_____

Commandment 12:   Matthew 22:39 (KJV)

Explain why commandment 12 is important.

_____

_____

_____

_____

_____

_____

How will you apply this verse to your personal life?

_____

_____

_____

_____

_____

_____

How will you apply this verse to your relationship with your wife?

_____

_____

_____

_____

_____

_____

Glorify 1: Proverbs 3:9 (KJV)

Explain why commandment glorify 1 is important.

How will you apply this verse to your personal life?

How will you apply this verse to your relationship with your wife?

Glorify 2: 2 Chronicles 20:21 (KJV)

Explain why glorify 2 is important.

_____

_____

_____

_____

_____

_____

How will you apply this verse to your personal life?

_____

_____

_____

_____

_____

_____

How will you apply this verse to your relationship with your wife?

_____

_____

_____

_____

_____

_____

Glorify 3A: John 4:23 (KJV)

Explain why glorify 3A is important.

_____

_____

_____

_____

_____

_____

How will you apply this verse to your personal life?

_____

_____

_____

_____

_____

How will you apply this verse to your relationship with your wife?

_____

_____

_____

_____

_____

_____

Glorify 3B: John 4:24 (KJV)

Explain why glorify 3B is important.

_____

_____

_____

_____

_____

_____

How will you apply this verse to your personal life?

_____

_____

_____

_____

_____

_____

How will you apply this verse to your relationship with your wife?

_____

_____

_____

_____

_____

_____

Chapter 5 verses

Behold, the days come, saith the LORD, that I will make a new covenant with the house of Israel, and with the house of Judah: Not according to the covenant that I made with their fathers in the day that I took them by the hand to bring them out of the land of Egypt; which my covenant they brake, although I was an husband unto them, saith the LORD: But this shall be the covenant that I will make with the house of Israel; After those days, saith the LORD, I will put my law in their inward parts, and write it in their hearts; and will be their God, and they shall be my people. And they shall teach no more every man his neighbour, and every man his brother, saying, Know the LORD: for they shall all know me, from the least of them unto the greatest of them, saith the LORD: for I will forgive their iniquity, and I will remember their sin no more. Thus saith the LORD, which giveth the sun for a light by day, and the ordinances of the moon and of the stars for a light by night, which divideth the sea when the waves thereof roar; The LORD of hosts is his name: If those ordinances depart from before me, saith the LORD, then the seed of Israel also shall cease from being a nation before me for ever. Thus saith the LORD; If heaven above can be measured, and the foundations of the earth searched out beneath, I will also cast off all the seed of Israel for all that they have done, saith the LORD (Jeremiah 31:31- 37 KJV).

Husband Leadership Principle # 4

Husbands, love your wives, and be not bitter against them (Colossians 3:19 KJV).

Communication is the fourth leadership behavior that husbands must exhibit. Husbands who communicate that they are the image of God and that they glorify God will enhance their wives perception of them. Any communication that enhances the wives perception of the husband will also enhance their marriage. Without developing a communication plan the husband could place himself in a dilemma with his wife that will continue with the characteristics of a dysfunctional marriage.

In Isaiah 6:9, God warned His prophet of the dilemma involved in communicating with other people. God knows that people may hear you speak but for many reasons may not understand the purpose of your communication.

And he said, Go, and tell this people, Hear ye indeed, but understand not; and see ye indeed, but perceive not (Isaiah 6:9).

It will benefit the husband to have a process where they can evaluate how the way that they talk impacts their communication. Both Laban and Judas could have benefited from a process that evaluates how the way that they talk impacts their communication to others.

The first phase in the process is to move our complaints to commitments. You must begin by deciding what must happen more frequently. Next you must decide what must happen more frequently for you to attain this commitment. Finally, you evaluate what is your commitment.

In Genesis 30:25-31 Jacob requested that Laban allow him to return home. Laban, who was the leader of the family, responded by telling Jacob that he and his family had been blessed due to Jacobs's existence in the family and that he would give him the wages that Jacob demanded.

Jacob felt that he must have additional cattle before he departed. To have more cattle means that his cattle would have to produce more cattle. Producing more cattle would provide Jacob the resources necessary for him to provide for his family so that he could move to his own country. Jacobs's complaint was when shall I provide for my family without your support. This translates into a commitment to be the provider and leader of his family.

The second phase is to move from blame to personal responsibility. Jacob blamed Laban for his present circumstance which did not allow him to become the leader of his family. In order to become the leader of his family he implemented a plan that would increase his number of sheep. He began by selecting a very small flock and then implemented a plan given to him by God.

And Jacob took him rods of green poplar, and of the hazel and chesnut tree; and pilled white strakes in them, and made the white appear which was in the rods. And he set the rods which he had pilled before the flocks in the gutters in the watering troughs when the flocks came to drink, that they should conceive when they came to drink. And the flocks conceived before the rods, and brought forth cattle ringstraked, speckled, and spotted. And Jacob did separate the lambs, and set the faces of the flocks toward the ringstraked, and all the brown in the flock of Laban; and he put his own flocks by themselves, and put them not unto Laban's cattle. And it came to pass, whensoever the stronger cattle did conceive, that Jacob laid the rods before the eyes of the cattle in the gutters, that they might conceive among the rods. But when the cattle were feeble, he put them not in: so the feebler were Laban's, and the stronger Jacob's. And the man increased exceedingly, and had much cattle, and maidservants, and menservants, and camels, and asses (Genesis 30:37- 43).

The third phase is to move from competing commitments to new resolutions. To move into this phase you must evaluate what fears or discomforts that keep you from accomplishing your intended commitment. Genesis 31:1 - 20, reveals that Jacob had become afraid of Laban and his sons. God had allowed a wealth transfer from the family of Laban to the family of Jacob. This created a natural competition to his commitment to provide for his family. The resolution was for him to move his family from the presence of the Laban clan as God had directed.

The final phase is to determine the assumption that you held. In the third phase Jacob feared that as long as he was dependent on Laban that he would not be able to provide for his family. Therefore he assumed that as long as he was independent of Laban that he would be able to provide for his family. Now if he had communicated that in the beginning, the afterward events would have been different. In Genesis 29:15 Laban asked Jacob what shall I pay you for your wages? If Jacob had told him that my ultimate goal is to provide for my family. Maybe Laban would have given him his wages along with the family. Instead Jacob told Laban that he wanted to increase the quantity of flock that he possessed.

I will pass through all thy flock to day, removing from thence all the speckled and spotted cattle, and all the brown cattle among the sheep, and the spotted and speckled among the goats: and of such shall be my hire (Genesis 30:32).

Another example is Judas Iscariot, the disciple who betrayed Jesus. In Matthew 27:3 - 4, Judas stated that he had sinned and betrayed innocent blood.

Then Judas, which had betrayed him, when he saw that he was condemned, repented himself, and brought again the thirty pieces of silver to the chief priests and elders, Saying, I have sinned in that I have betrayed the innocent blood. And they said, What is that to us? see thou to that. And he cast down the pieces of silver in the temple, and departed, and went and hanged himself (Mat 27:3 – 5).

Judas complained that he had betrayed innocent blood. His commitment indicates that he wanted innocent people to be betrayed less often if not at all. This moves his complaint to his commitment. He accepted 30 shillings of silver for this deed. What kept him from accomplishing his commitment was greed for money. The estimated value of 30 shillings of silver is the price of a small farm or $240,000. His greed was keeping him from meeting his commitment of not betraying innocent people. He probably feared becoming a poor person. So his assumption may have been that If I accept the thirty shillings of silver I will not become poor. If he had communicated his desire to be rich he would have known that participating in a plot to murder someone will not make you rich but only give you a ticket to hell.

On the next page you will complete the activities associated with husband leadership principle #4.

Now it is your turn. List your top ten complaints that you have about your wife.

Complaint

1.	
2.	
3.	
4.	
5.	
6.	
7.	
8.	
9.	
10.	

167

Complaint # 1: Write the first complaint that you listed in the previous table on the lines below.

_____

_____

_____

What would have to happen more often to reduce this complaint? Or what would have to happen less often to reduce this complaint.

_____

_____

_____

What does this reveal about your commitment?

_____

_____

_____

Now fill in the blank to the following statement: I am committed to_____.

Secondly, what are you doing or not doing which is keeping you from accomplishing your commitment?

_____

_____

_____

Thirdly, what fears or discomforts do you have that keep you from accomplishing your commitment?

_____

_____

_____

Finally, you need to determine your assumption. Take your third statement and if it is negative write it as a positive statement. If it is positive, write it as a negative statement. For example if you have the following negative statement transforms it as follows

Statement 1: They never let me finish talking.
Statement 2: They always let me finish talking.

_____

_____

_____

Complaint # 2: Write the first complaint that you listed in the previous table on the lines below.
_____
_____
_____

What would have to happen more often to reduce this complaint? Or what would have to happen less often to reduce this complaint.
_____
_____
_____

What does this reveal about your commitment?
_____
_____
_____

Now fill in the blank to the following statement: I am committed to_____.

Secondly, what are you doing or not doing which is keeping you from accomplishing your commitment?
_____
_____
_____

Thirdly, what fears or discomforts do you have that keep you from accomplishing your commitment?

_____

_____

_____

Finally, you need to determine your assumption. Take your third statement and if it is negative write it as a positive statement. If it is positive, write it as a negative statement. For example if you have the following negative statement transforms it as follows

Statement 1: They never let me finish talking.
Statement 2: They always let me finish talking.

_____

_____

_____

Complaint # 3: Write the first complaint that you listed in the previous table on the lines below.
_____
_____
_____

What would have to happen more often to reduce this complaint? Or what would have to happen less often to reduce this complaint.
_____
_____
_____

What does this reveal about your commitment?
_____
_____
_____

Now fill in the blank to the following statement: I am committed to_____.

Secondly, what are you doing or not doing which is keeping you from accomplishing your commitment?
_____
_____
_____

Thirdly, what fears or discomforts do you have that keep you from accomplishing your commitment?

_____

_____

_____

Finally, you need to determine your assumption. Take your third statement and if it is negative write it as a positive statement. If it is positive, write it as a negative statement. For example if you have the following negative statement transforms it as follows

Statement 1: They never let me finish talking.
Statement 2: They always let me finish talking.

_____

_____

_____

Complaint # 4: Write the first complaint that you listed in the previous table on the lines below.

_____

_____

_____

What would have to happen more often to reduce this complaint? Or what would have to happen less often to reduce this complaint.

_____

_____

_____

What does this reveal about your commitment?

_____

_____

_____

Now fill in the blank to the following statement: I am committed to_____.

Secondly, what are you doing or not doing which is keeping you from accomplishing your commitment?

_____

_____

_____

Thirdly, what fears or discomforts do you have that keep you from accomplishing your commitment?

_____

_____

_____

Finally, you need to determine your assumption. Take your third statement and if it is negative write it as a positive statement. If it is positive, write it as a negative statement. For example if you have the following negative statement transforms it as follows

Statement 1: They never let me finish talking.
Statement 2: They always let me finish talking.

_____

_____

_____

Complaint # 5: Write the first complaint that you listed in the previous table on the lines below.

_____

_____

_____

What would have to happen more often to reduce this complaint? Or what would have to happen less often to reduce this complaint.

_____

_____

_____

What does this reveal about your commitment?

_____

_____

_____

Now fill in the blank to the following statement: I am committed to_____.

Secondly, what are you doing or not doing which is keeping you from accomplishing your commitment?

_____

_____

_____

Thirdly, what fears or discomforts do you have that keep you from accomplishing your commitment?

_____

_____

_____

Finally, you need to determine your assumption. Take your third statement and if it is negative write it as a positive statement. If it is positive, write it as a negative statement. For example if you have the following negative statement transforms it as follows

Statement 1: They never let me finish talking.
Statement 2: They always let me finish talking.

_____

_____

_____

Complaint # 6: Write the first complaint that you listed in the previous table on the lines below.

_____

_____

_____

What would have to happen more often to reduce this complaint? Or what would have to happen less often to reduce this complaint.

_____

_____

_____

What does this reveal about your commitment?

_____

_____

_____

Now fill in the blank to the following statement: I am committed to_____.

Secondly, what are you doing or not doing which is keeping you from accomplishing your commitment?

_____

_____

_____

Thirdly, what fears or discomforts do you have that keep you from accomplishing your commitment?

_____

_____

_____

Finally, you need to determine your assumption. Take your third statement and if it is negative write it as a positive statement. If it is positive, write it as a negative statement. For example if you have the following negative statement transforms it as follows

Statement 1: They never let me finish talking.
Statement 2: They always let me finish talking.

_____

_____

_____

Complaint # 7: Write the first complaint that you listed in the previous table on the lines below.

_____

_____

_____

What would have to happen more often to reduce this complaint? Or what would have to happen less often to reduce this complaint.

_____

_____

_____

What does this reveal about your commitment?

_____

_____

_____

Now fill in the blank to the following statement: I am committed to_____.

Secondly, what are you doing or not doing which is keeping you from accomplishing your commitment?

_____

_____

_____

Thirdly, what fears or discomforts do you have that keep you from accomplishing your commitment?

_____

_____

_____

Finally, you need to determine your assumption. Take your third statement and if it is negative write it as a positive statement. If it is positive, write it as a negative statement. For example if you have the following negative statement transforms it as follows

Statement 1: They never let me finish talking.
Statement 2: They always let me finish talking.

_____

_____

_____

Complaint # 8: Write the first complaint that you listed in the previous table on the lines below.

_____

_____

_____

What would have to happen more often to reduce this complaint? Or what would have to happen less often to reduce this complaint.

_____

_____

_____

What does this reveal about your commitment?

_____

_____

_____

Now fill in the blank to the following statement: I am committed to_____.

Secondly, what are you doing or not doing which is keeping you from accomplishing your commitment?

_____

_____

_____

Thirdly, what fears or discomforts do you have that keep you from accomplishing your commitment?

_____

_____

_____

Finally, you need to determine your assumption. Take your third statement and if it is negative write it as a positive statement. If it is positive, write it as a negative statement. For example if you have the following negative statement transforms it as follows

Statement 1: They never let me finish talking.
Statement 2: They always let me finish talking.

_____

_____

_____

Complaint # 9: Write the first complaint that you listed in the previous table on the lines below.
_____

_____

_____

What would have to happen more often to reduce this complaint? Or what would have to happen less often to reduce this complaint.

_____

_____

_____

What does this reveal about your commitment?

_____

_____

_____

Now fill in the blank to the following statement: I am committed to_____.

Secondly, what are you doing or not doing which is keeping you from accomplishing your commitment?

_____

_____

_____

Thirdly, what fears or discomforts do you have that keep you from accomplishing your commitment?

_____

_____

_____

Finally, you need to determine your assumption. Take your third statement and if it is negative write it as a positive statement. If it is positive, write it as a negative statement. For example if you have the following negative statement transforms it as follows

Statement 1: They never let me finish talking.
Statement 2: They always let me finish talking.

_____

_____

_____

Complaint # 10: Write the first complaint that you listed in the previous table on the lines below.

_____
_____
_____

What would have to happen more often to reduce this complaint? Or what would have to happen less often to reduce this complaint.

_____
_____
_____

What does this reveal about your commitment?

_____
_____
_____

Now fill in the blank to the following statement: I am committed to_____.

Secondly, what are you doing or not doing which is keeping you from accomplishing your commitment?

_____
_____
_____

Thirdly, what fears or discomforts do you have that keep you from accomplishing your commitment?

_____

_____

_____

Finally, you need to determine your assumption. Take your third statement and if it is negative write it as a positive statement. If it is positive, write it as a negative statement. For example if you have the following negative statement transforms it as follows

Statement 1: They never let me finish talking.
Statement 2: They always let me finish talking.

_____

_____

_____

Next you will develop a plan for communicating the image of God and to glorify God.

When God decided that He would deliver the Israelites from the hands of the Pharaoh, He understood that the Egyptians would hear Moses but refuse to cooperate because the Pharaoh would not understand. God communicated to the Egyptians and Israelites by using animals, blood, humans, and weather (Exodus 7:19-11:5). He uses dreams, visions, and prophets too.

Like God, effective husbands must use a variety of methods to communicate to their wives. The husband who decides to counterbalance the communication dysfunctions in his marriage must also use a variety of methods to communicate the twelve primary commandments and the glory of God. Leadership principal #2 required the reader to complete an extensive study of the twelve commandments and has therefore prepared the leader to facilitate communication activities for each of the twelve commandments and to glorify God. In the following activity, you will develop communication activities for each commandment. If necessary, review husband leadership principle #2 to help you complete the following activities.

Commandment 1:   Exodus 20:3 KJV

Activity	Activity Type
1.	
2.	
3.	
4.	
5.	
6.	
7.	
8.	
9.	
10.	

Commandment 2:   Exodus 20:4-6 KJV

Activity	Activity Type
1.	
2.	
3.	
4.	
5.	
6.	
7.	
8.	
9.	
10.	

Commandment 3:   Exodus 20:7 KJV

Activity	Activity Type
1.	
2.	
3.	
4.	
5.	
6.	
7.	
8.	
9.	
10.	

Commandment 4:   Exodus 20:8-11 KJV

Activity	Activity Type
1.	
2.	
3.	
4.	
5.	
6.	
7.	
8.	
9.	
10.	

Commandment 5:   Exodus 20:12 KJV

Activity	Activity Type
1.	
2.	
3.	
4.	
5.	
6.	
7.	
8.	
9.	
10.	

Commandment 6:   Exodus 20:13 KJV

Activity	Activity Type
1.	
2.	
3.	
4.	
5.	
6.	
7.	
8.	
9.	
10.	

Commandment 7:   Exodus 20:14 KJV

Activity	Activity Type
1.	
2.	
3.	
4.	
5.	
6.	
7.	
8.	
9.	
10.	

Commandment 8:   Exodus 20:15 KJV

Activity	Activity Type
1.	
2.	
3.	
4.	
5.	
6.	
7.	
8.	
9.	
10.	

Commandment 9:   Exodus 20:16 KJV

Activity	Activity Type
1.	
2.	
3.	
4.	
5.	
6.	
7.	
8.	
9.	
10.	

Commandment 10:   Exodus 20:17 KJV

Activity	Activity Type
1.	
2.	
3.	
4.	
5.	
6.	
7.	
8.	
9.	
10.	

Commandment 11: Matthew 22:37 (KJV)

Activity	Activity Type
1.	
2.	
3.	
4.	
5.	
6.	
7.	
8.	
9.	
10.	

Commandment 12: Matthew 22:39 (KJV)

Activity	Activity Type
1.	
2.	
3.	
4.	
5.	
6.	
7.	
8.	
9.	
10.	

Glorify 1:   **Proverbs 3:9 (KJV)**

Activity	Activity Type
1.	
2.	
3.	
4.	
5.	
6.	
7.	
8.	
9.	
10.	

Glorify 2: 2 Chronicles 20:21 (KJV)

Activity	Activity Type
1.	
2.	
3.	
4.	
5.	
6.	
7.	
8.	
9.	
10.	

Glorify 3A: John 4:23 (KJV)

Activity	Activity Type
1.	
2.	
3.	
4.	
5.	
6.	
7.	
8.	
9.	
10.	

Glorify 3B: John 4:24 (KJV)

Activity	Activity Type
1.	
2.	
3.	
4.	
5.	
6.	
7.	
8.	
9.	
10.	

Chapter 6 verses

Gen 30:25-31

And it came to pass, when Rachel had born Joseph, that Jacob said unto Laban, Send me away, that I may go unto mine own place, and to my country. Give me my wives and my children, for whom I have served thee, and let me go: for thou knowest my service which I have done thee. And Laban said unto him, I pray thee, if I have found favour in thine eyes, tarry: for I have learned by experience that the LORD hath blessed me for thy sake. And he said, Appoint me thy wages, and I will give it. And he said unto him, Thou knowest how I have served thee, and how thy cattle was with me. For it was little which thou hadst before I came, and it is now increased unto a multitude; and the LORD hath blessed thee since my coming: and now when shall I provide for mine own house also? And he said, What shall I give thee? And Jacob said, Thou shalt not give me any thing: if thou wilt do this thing for me, I will again feed and keep thy flock:

Gen 31:1 – 20

And he heard the words of Laban's sons, saying, Jacob hath taken away all that was our father's; and of that which was our father's hath he gotten all this glory. And Jacob beheld the countenance of Laban, and, behold, it was not toward him as before. And the LORD said unto Jacob, Return unto the land of thy fathers, and to thy kindred; and I will be with thee. And Jacob sent and called Rachel and Leah to the field unto his flock, And said unto them, I see your father's countenance, that it is not toward me as before; but the God of my father hath been with me. And ye know that with all my power I have served your father. And your father hath deceived me, and changed my wages ten times; but God suffered him not to hurt me. If he said thus, The speckled shall be thy wages; then all the cattle bare speckled: and if he said thus, The ringstraked shall be thy hire; then bare all the cattle ringstraked. Thus God hath taken away the cattle of your father, and given them to me. And it came to pass at the time that the cattle conceived, that I lifted up mine eyes, and saw in a dream, and, behold, the rams which leaped upon the cattle were ringstraked, speckled, and grisled. And the angel of God spake unto me in a dream, saying, Jacob: And I said, Here am I. And he said, Lift up now thine eyes, and see, all the rams which leap upon the cattle are ringstraked, speckled, and grisled: for I have seen all that Laban doeth unto thee. I am the God of Bethel, where thou anointedst the pillar, and where thou vowedst a vow unto me: now arise, get thee out from this land, and return unto the land of thy kindred. And Rachel and Leah answered and said unto him, Is there yet any portion or inheritance for us in our father's house? Are we not counted of him strangers? for he hath sold us, and hath quite devoured also our money. For all the riches which God hath taken from our father, that is ours, and our children's: now then, whatsoever God hath said unto thee, do. Then Jacob rose up, and set his sons and his wives upon camels; And he carried away all his cattle, and all his goods which he had gotten, the cattle of his getting, which he had gotten in Padanaram, for to go to Isaac his father in the land of Canaan. And Laban went to shear his sheep: and Rachel had stolen the images that were her father's. And Jacob stole away unawares to Laban the Syrian, in that he told him not that he fled.

Exodus 7

And the LORD said unto Moses, See, I have made thee a god to Pharaoh: and Aaron thy brother shall be thy prophet. Thou shalt speak all that I command thee: and Aaron thy brother shall speak unto Pharaoh, that he send the children of Israel out of his land. And I will harden Pharaoh's heart, and multiply my signs and my wonders in the land of Egypt. But Pharaoh shall not hearken unto you, that I may lay my hand upon Egypt, and bring forth mine armies, and my people the children of Israel, out of the land of Egypt by great judgments. And the Egyptians shall know that I am the LORD, when I stretch forth mine hand upon Egypt, and bring out the children of Israel from among them. And Moses and Aaron did as the LORD commanded them, so did they. And Moses was fourscore years old, and Aaron fourscore and three years old, when they spake unto Pharaoh. And the LORD spake unto Moses and unto Aaron, saying, When Pharaoh shall speak unto you, saying, Show a miracle for you: then thou shalt say unto Aaron, Take thy rod, and cast it before Pharaoh, and it shall become a serpent. And Moses and Aaron went in unto Pharaoh, and they did so as the LORD had commanded: and Aaron cast down his rod before Pharaoh, and before his servants, and it became a serpent. Then Pharaoh also called the wise men and the sorcerers: now the magicians of Egypt, they also did in like manner with their enchantments. For they cast down every man his rod, and they became serpents: but Aaron's rod swallowed up their rods. And he hardened Pharaoh's heart, that he hearkened not unto them; as the LORD had said. And the LORD said unto Moses, Pharaoh's heart is hardened, he refuseth to let the people go. Get thee unto Pharaoh in the morning; lo, he goeth out unto the water; and thou shalt stand by the river's brink against he come; and the rod which was turned to a serpent shalt thou take in thine hand. And thou shalt say unto him, The LORD God of the Hebrews hath sent me unto thee, saying, Let my people go, that they may serve me in the wilderness: and, behold, hitherto thou wouldest not hear. Thus saith the LORD, In this thou shalt know that I am the LORD: behold, I will smite with the rod that is in mine hand upon the waters which are in the river, and they shall be turned to blood. And the fish that is in the river shall die, and the river shall stink; and the Egyptians shall loathe to drink of the water of the river. And the LORD spake unto Moses, Say unto Aaron, Take thy rod, and stretch out thine hand upon the waters of Egypt, upon their streams, upon their rivers, and upon their ponds, and upon all their pools of water, that they may become blood; and that there may be blood throughout all the land of Egypt, both in vessels of wood, and in vessels of stone. And Moses and Aaron did so, as the LORD commanded; and he lifted up the rod, and smote the waters that were in the river, in the sight of Pharaoh, and in the sight of his servants; and all the waters that were in the river were turned to blood. And the fish that was in the river died; and the river stank, and the Egyptians could not drink of the water of the river; and there was blood throughout all the land of Egypt. And the magicians of Egypt did so with their enchantments: and Pharaoh's heart was hardened, neither did he hearken unto them; as the LORD had said. And Pharaoh turned and went into his house, neither did he set his heart to this also. And all the Egyptians digged round about the river for water to drink; for they could not drink of the water of the river. And seven days were fulfilled, after that the LORD had smitten the river.

Exodus 8

And the LORD spake unto Moses, Go unto Pharaoh, and say unto him, Thus saith the LORD, Let my people go, that they may serve me. And if thou refuse to let them go, behold, I will smite all thy borders with frogs: And the river shall bring forth frogs abundantly, which shall go up and come into thine house, and into thy bedchamber, and upon thy bed, and into the house of thy servants, and upon thy people, and into thine ovens, and into thy kneadingtroughs: And the frogs shall come up both on thee, and upon thy people, and upon all thy servants. And the LORD spake unto Moses, Say unto Aaron, Stretch forth thine hand with thy rod over the streams, over the rivers, and over the ponds, and cause frogs to come up upon the land of Egypt. And Aaron stretched out his hand over the waters of Egypt; and the frogs came up, and covered the land of Egypt. And the magicians did so with their enchantments, and brought up frogs upon the land of Egypt. Then Pharaoh called for Moses and Aaron, and said, Entreat the LORD, that he may take away the frogs from me, and from my people; and I will let the people go, that they may do sacrifice unto the LORD. And Moses said unto Pharaoh, Glory over me: when shall I entreat for thee, and for thy servants, and for thy people, to destroy the frogs from thee and thy houses, that they may remain in the river only? And he said, To morrow. And he said, Be it according to thy word: that thou mayest know that there is none like unto the LORD our God. And the frogs shall depart from thee, and from thy houses, and from thy servants, and from thy people; they shall remain in the river only. And Moses and Aaron went out from Pharaoh: and Moses cried unto the LORD because of the frogs which he had brought against Pharaoh. And the LORD did according to the word of Moses; and the frogs died out of the houses, out of the villages, and out of the fields. And they gathered them together upon heaps: and the land stank. But when Pharaoh saw that there was respite, he hardened his heart, and hearkened not unto them; as the LORD had said. And the LORD said unto Moses, Say unto Aaron, Stretch out thy rod, and smite the dust of the land, that it may become lice throughout all the land of Egypt. And they did so; for Aaron stretched out his hand with his rod, and smote the dust of the earth, and it became lice in man, and in beast; all the dust of the land became lice throughout all the land of Egypt. And the magicians did so with their enchantments to bring forth lice, but they could not: so there were lice upon man, and upon beast. Then the magicians said unto Pharaoh, This is the finger of God: and Pharaoh's heart was hardened, and he hearkened not unto them; as the LORD had said. And the LORD said unto Moses, Rise up early in the morning, and stand before Pharaoh; lo, he cometh forth to the water; and say unto him, Thus saith the LORD, Let my people go, that they may serve me. Else, if thou wilt not let my people go, behold, I will send swarms of flies upon thee, and upon thy servants, and upon thy people, and into thy houses: and the houses of the Egyptians shall be full of swarms of flies, and also the ground whereon they are. And I will sever in that day the land of Goshen, in which my people dwell, that no swarms of flies shall be there; to the end thou mayest know that I am the LORD in the midst of the earth. And I will put a division between my people and thy people: to morrow shall this sign be. And the LORD did so; and there came a grievous swarm of flies into the house of Pharaoh, and into his servants' houses, and into all the land of Egypt: the land was corrupted by reason of the swarm of flies. And Pharaoh called for Moses and for Aaron, and said, Go ye, sacrifice to your God in the land. And Moses said, It is not meet so to do; for we shall sacrifice the abomination of the Egyptians to the LORD our God: lo, shall we sacrifice the abomination of the Egyptians before their eyes, and will they not stone us? We will go three days' journey into the wilderness, and sacrifice to the LORD our God, as he shall command us. And Pharaoh said, I will let you go, that ye may sacrifice to the LORD your God in the wilderness; only ye shall not go very far away: entreat for me. And Moses said, Behold, I go out from thee, and I will entreat the LORD that the swarms of flies may depart from Pharaoh, from his servants, and from his people, to morrow: but let not Pharaoh deal deceitfully any more in not letting the people go to sacrifice to the LORD. And Moses went out from Pharaoh, and entreated the LORD. And the LORD did according to the word of Moses; and he removed the swarms of flies from Pharaoh, from his servants, and from his people; there remained not one. And Pharaoh hardened his heart at this time also, neither would he let the people go.

Exodus 9

Then the LORD said unto Moses, Go in unto Pharaoh, and tell him, Thus saith the LORD God of the Hebrews, Let my people go, that they may serve me. For if thou refuse to let them go, and wilt hold them still, Behold, the hand of the LORD is upon thy cattle which is in the field, upon the horses, upon the asses, upon the camels, upon the oxen, and upon the sheep: there shall be a very grievous murrain. And the LORD shall sever between the cattle of Israel and the cattle of Egypt: and there shall nothing die of all that is the children's of Israel. And the LORD appointed a set time, saying, To morrow the LORD shall do this thing in the land. And the LORD did that thing on the morrow, and all the cattle of Egypt died: but of the cattle of the children of Israel died not one. And Pharaoh sent, and, behold, there was not one of the cattle of the Israelites dead. And the heart of Pharaoh was hardened, and he did not let the people go. And the LORD said unto Moses and unto Aaron, Take to you handfuls of ashes of the furnace, and let Moses sprinkle it toward the heaven in the sight of Pharaoh. And it shall become small dust in all the land of Egypt, and shall be a boil breaking forth with blains upon man, and upon beast, throughout all the land of Egypt. And they took ashes of the furnace, and stood before Pharaoh; and Moses sprinkled it up toward heaven; and it became a boil breaking forth with blains upon man, and upon beast. And the magicians could not stand before Moses because of the boils; for the boil was upon the magicians, and upon all the Egyptians. And the LORD hardened the heart of Pharaoh, and he hearkened not unto them; as the LORD had spoken unto Moses. And the LORD said unto Moses, Rise up early in the morning, and stand before Pharaoh, and say unto him, Thus saith the LORD God of the Hebrews, Let my people go, that they may serve me. For I will at this time send all my plagues upon thine heart, and upon thy servants, and upon thy people; that thou mayest know that there is none like me in all the earth. For now I will stretch out my hand, that I may smite thee and thy people with pestilence; and thou shalt be cut off from the earth. And in very deed for this cause have I raised thee up, for to show in thee my power; and that my name may be declared throughout all the earth. As yet exaltest thou thyself against my people, that thou wilt not let them go? Behold, to morrow about this time I will cause it to rain a very grievous hail, such as hath not been in Egypt since the foundation thereof even until now. Send therefore now, and gather thy cattle, and all that thou hast in the field; for upon every man and beast which shall be found in the field, and shall not be brought home, the hail shall come down upon them, and they shall die. He that feared the word of the LORD among the servants of Pharaoh made his servants and his cattle flee into the houses: And he that regarded not the word of the LORD left his servants and his cattle in the field. And the LORD said unto Moses, Stretch forth thine hand toward heaven, that there may be hail in all the land of Egypt, upon man, and upon beast, and upon every herb of the field, throughout the land of Egypt. And Moses stretched forth his rod toward heaven: and the LORD sent thunder and hail, and the fire ran along upon the ground; and the LORD rained hail upon the land of Egypt. So there was hail, and fire mingled with the hail, very grievous, such as there was none like it in all the land of Egypt since it became a nation. And the hail smote throughout all the land of Egypt all that was in the field, both man and beast; and the hail smote every herb of the field, and brake every tree of the field. Only in the land of Goshen, where the children of Israel were, was there no hail. And Pharaoh sent, and called for Moses and Aaron, and said unto them, I have sinned this time: the LORD is righteous, and I and my people are wicked. Entreat the LORD (for it is enough) that there be no more mighty thunderings and hail; and I will let you go, and ye shall stay no longer. And Moses said unto him, As soon as I am gone out of the city, I will spread abroad my hands unto the LORD; and the thunder shall cease, neither shall there be any more hail; that thou mayest know how that the earth is the LORD'S. But as for thee and thy servants, I know that ye will not yet fear the LORD God. And the flax and the barley was smitten: for the barley was in the ear, and the flax was bolled. But the wheat and the rie were not smitten: for they were not grown up. And Moses went out of the city from Pharaoh, and spread abroad his hands unto the LORD: and the thunders and hail ceased, and the rain was not poured upon the earth. And when Pharaoh saw that the rain and the hail and the thunders were ceased, he sinned yet more, and hardened his heart, he and his servants. [35]And the heart of Pharaoh was hardened, neither would he let the children of Israel go; as the LORD had spoken by Moses.

Exodus 10

And the LORD said unto Moses, Go in unto Pharaoh: for I have hardened his heart, and the heart of his servants, that I might show these my signs before him: And that thou mayest tell in the ears of thy son, and of thy son's son, what things I have wrought in Egypt, and my signs which I have done among them; that ye may know how that I am the LORD. And Moses and Aaron came in unto Pharaoh, and said unto him, Thus saith the LORD God of the Hebrews, How long wilt thou refuse to humble thyself before me? let my people go, that they may serve me. Else, if thou refuse to let my people go, behold, to morrow will I bring the locusts into thy coast: And they shall cover the face of the earth, that one cannot be able to see the earth: and they shall eat the residue of that which is escaped, which remaineth unto you from the hail, and shall eat every tree which groweth for you out of the field: And they shall fill thy houses, and the houses of all thy servants, and the houses of all the Egyptians; which neither thy fathers, nor thy fathers' fathers have seen, since the day that they were upon the earth unto this day. And he turned himself, and went out from Pharaoh. And Pharaoh's servants said unto him, How long shall this man be a snare unto us? let the men go, that they may serve the LORD their God: knowest thou not yet that Egypt is destroyed? And Moses and Aaron were brought again unto Pharaoh: and he said unto them, Go, serve the LORD your God: but who are they that shall go? And Moses said, We will go with our young and with our old, with our sons and with our daughters, with our flocks and with our herds will we go; for we must hold a feast unto the LORD. And he said unto them, Let the LORD be so with you, as I will let you go, and your little ones: look to it; for evil is before you. Not so: go now ye that are men, and serve the LORD; for that ye did desire. And they were driven out from Pharaoh's presence. And the LORD said unto Moses, Stretch out thine hand over the land of Egypt for the locusts, that they may come up upon the land of Egypt, and eat every herb of the land, even all that the hail hath left. And Moses stretched forth his rod over the land of Egypt, and the LORD brought an east wind upon the land all that day, and all that night; and when it was morning, the east wind brought the locusts. And the locusts went up over all the land of Egypt, and rested in all the coasts of Egypt: very grievous were they; before them there were no such locusts as they, neither after them shall be such. For they covered the face of the whole earth, so that the land was darkened; and they did eat every herb of the land, and all the fruit of the trees which the hail had left: and there remained not any green thing in the trees, or in the herbs of the field, through all the land of Egypt. Then Pharaoh called for Moses and Aaron in haste; and he said, I have sinned against the LORD your God, and against you. Now therefore forgive, I pray thee, my sin only this once, and entreat the LORD your God, that he may take away from me this death only. And he went out from Pharaoh, and entreated the LORD. And the LORD turned a mighty strong west wind, which took away the locusts, and cast them into the Red sea; there remained not one locust in all the coasts of Egypt. But the LORD hardened Pharaoh's heart, so that he would not let the children of Israel go. And the LORD said unto Moses, Stretch out thine hand toward heaven, that there may be darkness over the land of Egypt, even darkness which may be felt. And Moses stretched forth his hand toward heaven; and there was a thick darkness in all the land of Egypt three days: They saw not one another, neither rose any from his place for three days: but all the children of Israel had light in their dwellings. And Pharaoh called unto Moses, and said, Go ye, serve the LORD; only let your flocks and your herds be stayed: let your little ones also go with you. And Moses said, Thou must give us also sacrifices and burnt offerings, that we may sacrifice unto the LORD our God. Our cattle also shall go with us; there shall not an hoof be left behind; for thereof must we take to serve the LORD our God; and we know not with what we must serve the LORD, until we come thither. But the LORD hardened Pharaoh's heart, and he would not let them go. And Pharaoh said unto him, Get thee from me, take heed to thyself, see my face no more; for in that day thou seest my face thou shalt die. And Moses said, Thou hast spoken well, I will see thy face again no more.

Exodus 11: 1 – 5

And the LORD said unto Moses, Yet will I bring one plague more upon Pharaoh, and upon Egypt; afterwards he will let you go hence: when he shall let you go, he shall surely thrust you out hence altogether. Speak now in the ears of the people, and let every man borrow of his neighbour, and every woman of her neighbour, jewels of silver, and jewels of gold. And the LORD gave the people favour in the sight of the Egyptians. Moreover the man Moses was very great in the land of Egypt, in the sight of Pharaoh's servants, and in the sight of the people. And Moses said, Thus saith the LORD, About midnight will I go out into the midst of Egypt: And all the firstborn in the land of Egypt shall die, from the firstborn of Pharaoh that sitteth upon his throne, even unto the firstborn of the maidservant that is behind the mill; and all the firstborn of beasts.

Husband Leadership Principle # 5

Not as though I had already attained, either were already perfect: but I follow after, if that I may apprehend that for which also I am apprehended of Christ Jesus. Brethren, I count not myself to have apprehended: but this one thing I do, forgetting those things which are behind, and reaching forth unto those things which are before, I press toward the mark for the prize of the high calling of God in Christ Jesus (Philippians 3:12 - 14).

Self-discipline is the fifth leadership behavior that leaders must exhibit to complete the process that renders the dysfunctional marriage functional. Paul understood that discipline is required for leaders to accomplish the task that God has ordained for them to accomplish. In Corinthians 9:24-27, Paul emphasizes that in order to receive the prize we must train and stay the course.

Know ye not that they which run in a race run all, but one receiveth the prize? So run, that ye may obtain. And every man that striveth for the mastery is temperate in all things. Now they do it to obtain a corruptible crown; but we an incorruptible. I therefore so run, not as uncertainly; so fight I, not as one that beateth the air: But I keep under my body, and bring it into subjection: lest that by any means, when I have preached to others, I myself should be a castaway (1 Corinthians 9:24 – 27 KJV).

Staying the course will require planning for the husband who desires to render a dysfunctional marriage functional. In Husband Leadership Principle #1 you began this race with activities for each of the twelve primary commandments. In Husband Leadership Principle #2 you developed activities for setting the appropriate character for each primary commandment. In Husband Leadership Principle #3 you developed your commitment activities for each of the twelve primary commandments. In Husband Leadership Principle #4 you developed activities that would ensure that you effectively communicate the twelve primary commandments.

Developing the plan will provide the leader with the moral restraint, composure, and patience needed to remain disciplined through the transition. Now you will develop activities that will ensure that you exhibit the self-discipline needed to overcome the dysfunctional marraige. You will develop a plan of implementation for each primary commandment.

Commandment 1:   Exodus 20:3 KJV

Activity Type	Timeline (Daily, Weekly, Monthly, Yearly - Date(s))

Commandment 2: Exodus 20:4-6 KJV

Activity Type	Timeline (Daily, Weekly, Monthly, Yearly - Date(s))

Commandment 3:   Exodus 20:7 KJV

Activity Type	Timeline (Daily, Weekly, Monthly, Yearly - Date(s))

Commandment 4:   Exodus 20:8-11 KJV

Activity Type	Timeline (Daily, Weekly, Monthly, Yearly - Date(s))

Commandment 5:   Exodus 20:12 KJV

Activity Type	Timeline (Daily, Weekly, Monthly, Yearly - Date(s))

Commandment 6:   Exodus 20:13 KJV

Activity Type	Timeline (Daily, Weekly, Monthly, Yearly - Date(s))

Commandment 7:   Exodus 20:14 KJV

Activity Type	Timeline (Daily, Weekly, Monthly, Yearly - Date(s))

Commandment 8:   Exodus 20:15 KJV

Activity Type	Timeline (Daily, Weekly, Monthly, Yearly - Date(s))

Commandment 9:   Exodus 20:16 KJV

Activity Type	Timeline (Daily, Weekly, Monthly, Yearly - Date(s))

Commandment 10:   Exodus 20:17 KJV

Activity Type	Timeline (Daily, Weekly, Monthly, Yearly - Date(s))

Commandment 11: Matthew 22:37 (KJV).

Activity Type	Timeline (Daily, Weekly, Monthly, Yearly - Date(s))

Commandment 12:   Matthew 22:39 (KJV)

Activity Type	Timeline (Daily, Weekly, Monthly, Yearly - Date(s))

www.ingramcontent.com/pod-product-compliance
Lightning Source LLC
Chambersburg PA
CBHW080730230426
43665CB00020B/2688